To Betty with love! oo

Bilan

OCT 97

French Tulips,
Boston, 1992

To my wife Edna

ISBN 0-8263-1563-1

Designed by William Field, Santa Fe, NM

Typeset in Galliard by Mindy Holmes
at Copygraphics, Santa Fe, NM

Printed on Gardamatt Brilliante

Separations made by Arnoldo Mondadori Editore,
S.p.A., Verona, Italy

Printed and bound by Arnoldo Mondadori Editore,
S.p.A., Verona, Italy

THE
THIRD
EYE

TEXT BY SALLY EAUCLAIRE

YEAROUT EDITIONS • WESTON, MASSACHUSETTS

DISTRIBUTED BY
UNIVERSITY OF NEW MEXICO PRESS
ALBUQUERQUE

BÉLA KALMAN ■ A LIFETIME IN PHOTOGRAPHY

Mask from Bali with Deer Antlers, Santa Fe, 1987

*Kalman cut across cultures and continents to make this
shamanic image about the power of vision. To be fully whole, it
suggests we need to acknowledge both our light and shadow sides,
cultivate love (as seen in the heart shape), and see ourselves in
the context of infinity (represented by the double looped sign).*

INTRODUCTION ■ THE THIRD EYE

Béla Kalman often speaks of his "third eye." For more than 55 years he has used this intuitive, inner lens to see beyond the range of ordinary, everyday vision. It is the source of his imagination, creativity and new ideas. ■ With his two eyes Kalman *looks*. With his third eye he *sees*. The teamwork is essential. When looking, he recognizes photographic possibilities based on decades of past experience and knowledge. When seeing, he overrules his known ideas in favor of full, open experience in the here and now. ■ Ever curious, he has long explored diverse ways of seeing, from the peculiarly photographic one-eyed vision of the camera to the multi-eyed views of the Northwest totem pole carving people, who located eyes in the hands, feet, ears, joints, heart, bellies and groins of totemic animals to give them complete awareness. ■ Over the years, this photographer has explored worm's eye views, bird's eye views, peripheral vision, blurred vision, double vision, optical illusions and "fool the eye" games. He has looked from near, from far and from unexpected angles. In his studio he has had the most fun of all, conjuring kaleidoscopic arrays of shifting shapes, colors and perspectives.
■ The great street photographer Garry Winogrand once said he photographed "to see what something looks like when photographed." Kalman, too, regularly clicks the shutter at the blink of his third eye. Proud of being a "first impression photographer," he knows there is plenty of time later to consider philosophical ramifications and formal balances. Not every image must go into what he calls his "permanent collection." Those that do retain surprise and spontaneity. ■ Kalman also credits his third eye when images appear clearly imagined and indelibly registered in his brain. Transfering them to film is the challenge, one which he regards as a "real brain image gymnastic exercise." ■ A sleuth and strategist, he fervently believes that he can actualize what he visualizes. It is true of the photographs that he previsualizes with his third eye as well as of the life he envisions in his mind's eye. That said, the third eye and the mind's eye are not identical. The third eye is the home of instinct and intuition; the mind's eye of thought, attitude, mental perspective and world view. ■ For more than 55 years Béla Kalman has used his mind's eye to visualize success, sometimes against heavy odds. Consistently envisioning the world in the most positive terms possible—rather than through the distorting filters of preconception, bias, prejudice, greed and power—he has manifested harmony, happiness, joy and excitement in both his life and his photography.

Sally Eauclaire,
Santa Fe, February, 1994

**Fine Arts Museum Interior,
Budapest, Hungary, 1946**

*Kalman lay on the floor to make this
unusual photograph of pictures
within pictures, rooms within rooms
and a gameboard ceiling complete
with a dangling ball. The photograph
plays on the shared etymologies of the
words* room *and* camera, *with each
room of the museum functioning as
an enormous camera. The work can,
of course, be seen primarily as a post
World War II document of a
museum where visitors stayed bundled
up because there was no heat.*

2

Streetwork, 1940

*Although he'd only been photograph-
ing a year, Kalman noted the striking
silhouettes of these workers. Repairs on
Andrassy Boulevard, one of Budapest's
main thoroughfares, were always
done in the summer.*

Streetscene, Chicago, 1958
*Let the viewer decide whether this scene
represents Surrealist street theater, the
aftermath of an earthquake or business
as usual in the Windy City.*

4

Prudential Insurance Company Skyscraper, 1963

During his first winter in Boston, Kalman was intrigued by the sight of the city's first skyscraper under construction. Photographing it on his lunch hour, he caught the tower's metal skeleton in the deep fog, its top invisible and a pigeon flying in the foreground. "I waited patiently for the pigeon to fly in with its wings outstretched for landing." As an ad for Prudential, this photograph was seen around the world.

5

**Pole Painter, City Hall,
New York City, 1959**

*Béla looked out of the window of a
building in lower Manhattan and
spotted a fearless pole painter, who
began his work at the top with two
coats of paint and worked downward.*

**Windows in Montreux,
Switzerland, 1962**

*Kalman spotted this building
from a distance. When someone opened
the top window, he thought "perfect
sequence" and promptly shot it.*

***Abandoned School,
Brookline, MA, 1961***

*Grids organize and activate many of
Kalman's photographs, their rhythmic
patterns reaffirming his classical need
for formal beauty and order.*

Versailles, France, 1962

These eccentric and rickety chairs
seem divertingly out of step with the
highly ordered ostentation at
the 17th century palace of Versailles.

Paris Chimneys, 1962

Kalman found this maze of "pickup sticks" from the roof of Notre Dame Cathedral.

Mufflers, Boston, 1962

Like many modern artists, Kalman is enticed by the possibility of "rescuing" castoffs (such as this pile of discarded automobile mufflers) and recycling them into fresh, new artworks.

Village Scene, Bükk Region, Hungary, 1953

*Every evening the night watchman at a
state farm enjoyed a beer before reporting for
duty. Invariably, he was joined by a group
of horse handlers who had just completed
their hard day's work.*

Family Dinner, Chicago, 1957

On assignment for Life *magazine,*
Kalman criss-crossed the United States to
photograph Hungarian families that had
arrived in America a year earlier after the
failure of the 1956 revolution. Of the 13
children in this family, one child stayed
behind with a grandmother and 12 came to
America. A single lightbulb on the ceiling
was the sole source of light.

Sigismund Kisfaludy-Strobl at 70,
Budapest, 1953

After World War II this popular Hngarian
sculptor turned to socialist realism and was
richly rewarded by the government. His
many sitters included George Bernard Shaw
and Queen Elizabeth when she was still a
young princess. Kalman photographed the
sculptor around his 70th birthday—"a big
number for men living in Hungary."

**Joint Distribution Committee,
Budapest, 1946**

*The needy or elderly people waiting in front
of this bullet-ridden building await free
food distributed by an American agency. As
Kalman says, "The face of the lady in front
tells the entire sad story."*

Village Blacksmith, 1955
Bükk Mts., Hungary

Béla took this photograph of the village blacksmith while he was taking a break. This was one of many negatives that Kalman should have turned over to the state enterprise in 1951 after socialism forced him to close Kalman Foto. Instead he tucked it away and eventually brought it to America. The photograph won awards all over the globe.

16/17

Alfred Duca, Boston, 1964-65

*Kalman used the technique of double
exposure to make this portrait of Boston
artist Alfred Duca with the sculpture he
was commissioned to do for the Prudential
Insurance Company lobby.*

Horse Ranch, Bükk Mountains, 1955

Kalman didn't know it at the time, but parts of Hungary resemble America's Wild West. At a state-run farm, he spotted two-year old horses prancing around the corral, kicking up dust. Whereas other photographers would have seen only airborne dirt, he perceived the dust as a luminous screen that softens, lightens and indicates direction of movement.

Snowflakes' Dance, Budapest, 1954

During the 1940s and early 1950s, Kalman was a most successful ballet pho-tographer in Hungary. Photographing the Nutcracker Suite, *he used a tripod and slow shutter speed to catch the wispy "snow-flakes" twirling in motion. The dancers' legs stayed on the ground long enough to appear solid.*

Flames of Paris, 1955
A year before leaving Hungary, Kalman photographed these dancers on an open stage in Budapest. The photograph was included in Kalman's first picture book, a look at ballet in Hungary.

**Time Exposed Ballet,
New York City, 1958**

*Nora Kovach and Istvan Rab, solo dancers
with the Hungarian Ballet, escaped to
the West through the Berlin subway.
Kalman photographed them in New York
City, choosing them to make his first
multiple exposure photograph.
"Very new at that time," he says.*

Dame Margot Fonteyn, 1957

When Margot Fonteyn danced at the Chicago Civic Opera in Igor Stravinsky's Firebird, *Kalman decided to pose her dancing on a mirror to achieve the effect of a double image.*

Miraculous Mandarin, Budapest, 1955

This startling surreal photograph depicts the scene in Béla Bartok's ballet when three pimps point at a prostitute and order her to bring in the Mandarin, whom they plan to rob and kill.

Frida Kahlo, 1990

Kalman found Frida Kahlo's face—with its bushy eyebrows, sensuous mouth, and devouring, bewitching eyes—both unforgettable and photogenic. In this photogram he appropriated one of the Mexican painter's anguished self portraits and added veins to her skin with a fan coral. The dried plants represent her hard, thorny life, while the angel with a trumpet speaks of his hope that Kahlo and her husband Diego Rivera (shown painted in her mind's eye) now live peacefully in heaven.

Curious Bars, 1990
This eyepopping photogram combines a drawing by Hungarian-born op artist Victor Vasarely with a photograph of the American supermodel Cindy Crawford posed as yogi but looking like a sex goddess.

Shiko Munakata, Woodblock Carver,
New York City, 1959

Munakata at Work,
New York City, 1959

While on assignment for the New York
Times Magazine, *Kalman took these
photographs of Shiko Munakata, the
renowned Japanese woodcut artist. "He
was a small man under five feet, very
nearsighted with a very raspy voice," the
photographer remembers. For Munakata,
every calligraphic stroke had meaning.
His works were so popular in Japan that
they were reproduced in a twelve volume
set. Kalman shows two sides of this
artist: the busy, active artist functioning
in the world and the contemplative priest.*

**Bükk Mountain Scene,
Hungary, 1955**

*Seen from this low angle, the tall
beech trees dwarf the hikers. The
photographer thus turned an everyday
scene in the Bükk Mountains into
something provocative, unfamiliar,
even dreamlike and unreal.*

28

**Dusty Road,
Bükk Mountains,
Hungary, 1954**

*Everywhere Béla showed this
photograph people admired it;
it was the winner of the gold
medal at a FIAP exhibition
in Ijui, Brazil.*

Sunday in Florence, 1962

Ollas, Oaxaca, 1993

Zebras in Rome, 1962

Béla often enlivens pictures of routine events by choosing the dramatic camera angles, strong diagonals and bold, repeated patterns characteristic of "new vision" photography.

MY FRIEND, BÉLA

Béla Kalman was born in Hungary and as a young man earned a significant reputation in his field of fine photography. Historical events made him leave Hungary in October of 1956 and he settled in the US. ▦ It would not be an exaggeration to say that his joy in the visual world, his appetite for richness of his surroundings, his fresh discerning eye and his insatiable yearning for the beauties of the world have carried him far and wide. In spite of many perils and challenges he faced through the years, he always looked at the world with spirit and abundant confidence. Perhaps it is just this infectious pleasure in the curious surfaces of nature that helped him maintain his balance and in turn enabled him to produce such well composed images. ▦ Though the spectrum of his interest is varied and rich, his strongest pictures are those where he was truly enjoying nature's vistas. But Kalman doesn't close his eyes to the realities of this world. Guided by a warm heart, he constantly searches for ways to reveal hardship and blind alleys of this late 20th century. Because he sees in the deepest sense beyond the surfaces, his photographs are more than mere competent poetical facsimilies of reality, they are moving metaphors. ▦ His quiet but powerful images show the drama and the richness of our multicolored and infinite universe. In his native land, in the distant Southeast Asia, and also in the American Southwest. He shows us the people in their environment and gives us yet unknown features and details. Kalman has a rare sensitivity. Whether it is a balloon festival or Khmer temples or Mexican ruins, his images are fresh and flamboyant. As a professional photographer and making a living doing advertising photography, it is clear that he enjoys wholeheartedly both his professional career and also his creative work. ▦ I was lucky. I saw him as a pro taking pictures of me during several painting sessions in my Boston studio and in my Cape Cod summer home. He thought that he was watching me in my painting process, but it was I who watched him as he tried to catch me on film during my meditative painting session. He made himself almost invisible so as not to interfere with my progress. He did it with great sensitivity and the result was a series of well composed, exciting and candidly spontaneous photos of painting sessions from its inception to the finished piece over a six month period. ▦ I consider him my good friend; he always enjoyed my works and photographed most of them for the record for many years. He worked with many painters, sculptors, dancers, composers and I saw a number of sensitive and unique studies of others, some even from our old country. He enjoys experimentation and though not a young man anymore he always tries new ways and new processes. He travels widely and I listen with pleasure to his narrations and enjoy looking at the photos created on these trips. I consider Béla to be among the best of photo artists.

Kepes in Wellfleet, MA, 1977

Close-up of Gyorgy Kepes' Palette, Cambridge, MA, 1977

Gyorgy Kepes, Cambridge, June 1983.

An Orthodox Teenager, 1986

*Kalman couldn't resist
photographing this teenager
surveying the scene in the Mea
Shearim section of Jerusalem.*

**Fire Dance, Galisteo
Summer Festival, 1987**

*Recording the path of this fire
dancer, Kalman concentrated
on his impassioned,
dramatic, fiery essence.*

Oldtimer, Stockbridge, MA, 1989
*What should we make of this levitating
coffee table recycled from an ancient tree?
Is it amusing evidence of Yankee
ingenuity, a giant squashed amoeba,
or both? The funky butterfly chairs seem
to suggest that the wood has had a
fitting metamorphosis.*

Pigeon Summit on Fifth Avenue, 1989
Purposely exaggerating the
flattened space that naturally results
from the camera's monocular vision,
Kalman visually connected these lights,
poles and distant apartment building.

Two Bar Chairs, Brockton, MA, 1986

These reflections of bar chairs looked a bit tipsy when the photographer spotted them in the pool outside an art museum.

Road Signs in Tierra Nueva, Santa Fe, 1986

Fortunately, Kalman has never felt compelled to find the one and only true path in either photography or in life.

Archbishop Lamy in Santa Fe, 1990

*Lamy joins Béla's cast
of snow-clad ''plaster people''.
A powerful man with light and
dark sides, this 19th century priest
sought to balance his material
and spiritual sides.*

40

Streetscene in Santa Fe, 1986

The push/pull of colors in this photograph mimic the tug of past and present represented by this old-time pawn shop and its horseback riding and beetle driving clientele.

**Half and Half,
Brookline, MA 1982**

Kalman delights in the idiosyncrasies of ethnic neighborhoods. Here self assertion runs amok—or all American individualism lives—when families decorate their halves of a double house without accounting to each other.

42

Bermuda Triangle, 1980

*Vacationing in Bermuda, Béla
discovered a ''double-trouble'' version of
the mysterious Bermuda Triangle.*

43

Mary Rogers, Boston, 1971

In memory of his friend Mary
Rogers, who was a student of the great
Abstract Expressionist Hans
Hoffman, Kalman used one of her
paintings as a background for a floral
arrangement. Both painting and
flowers are reflected kaleidoscopically
on Mylar.

Some Avocado Pit, Boston, 1966

Béla catered this incredible non-edible
for a Boston jeweler's advertising
campaign. The chunky Australian
opal set in gold and clustered
diamonds came from the jeweler's
collection, the avocado from
Edna's kitchen.

44

**Steel Sculpture at Shidoni Gallery,
Tesuque, NM, 1985**

*Members of the public often treat the shiny
surfaces of polished stainless steel sculptures
as funhouse mirrors where they can mug
and pose. To make this photograph Kalman
took a different tack. Posing his wife, Edna,
as the backdrop, he set off the smooth
singing form of the sculpture as well as its
dancing reflections and mottled colors.*

**Shop Window, Bahnhofstrasse,
Zurich, 1988**

*In noting the surrealist nature of
photography, André Bazin described
photographs as "hallucinations
that are also facts." In this "still"
photograph, marked by rippling,
dreamlike layers of facts, patterns and
reflections, a "peeping tom" checks
out sextuplet mannequins.*

**Two Japanese Scenes,
near Kyoto, 1986**

*These understated views intimate the
power of natural forces hidden under
quiet surfaces. Paradoxically, the
circles embrace all, without beginning
or end, yet contain nothing and
frame the void.*

48

Bryce Canyon, Utah, 1987

Kalman visits Bryce Canyon to see spires, towers, steeples, battlements and other palatial natural wonders.

Lava Rings, Big Island, Hawaii, 1988
Mother Earth's braided hair is the work
of a world-class beautician—the Hawaiian
goddess Pele, whose volcanic eruptions
enlighten and empower all who worship her.

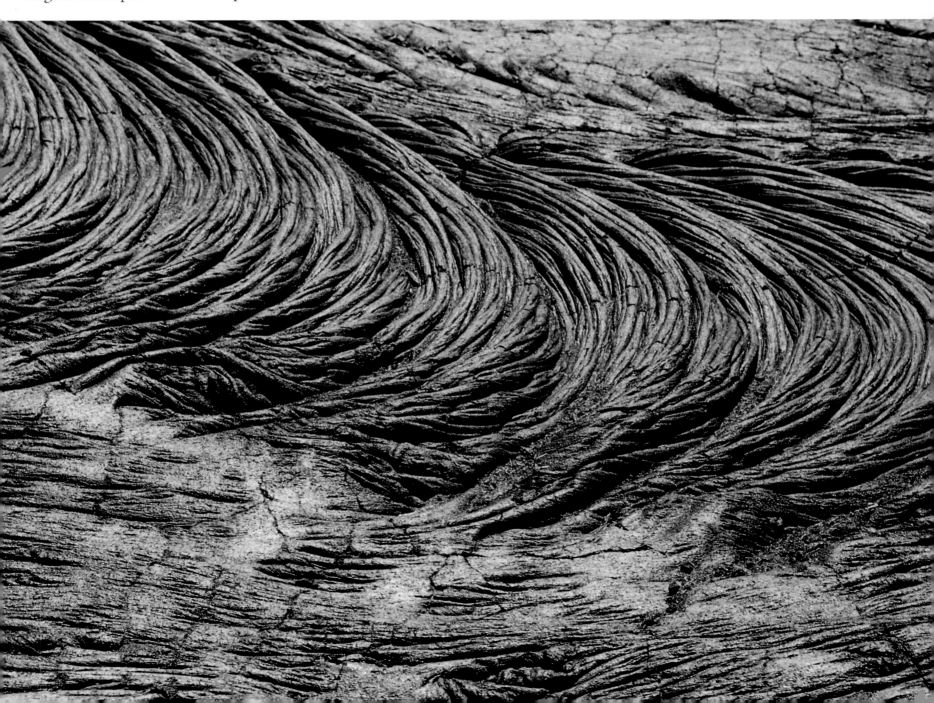

Streetcars, Kennebunkport, Maine, 19??

The Abstract Expressionist painting at right looks like a single flat surface but Kalman has fooled the eye. It's not a painting at all but two sides of an antique streetcar awaiting restoration. As for the jigsaw puzzle at left, it will take some clever piecing to put it back together.

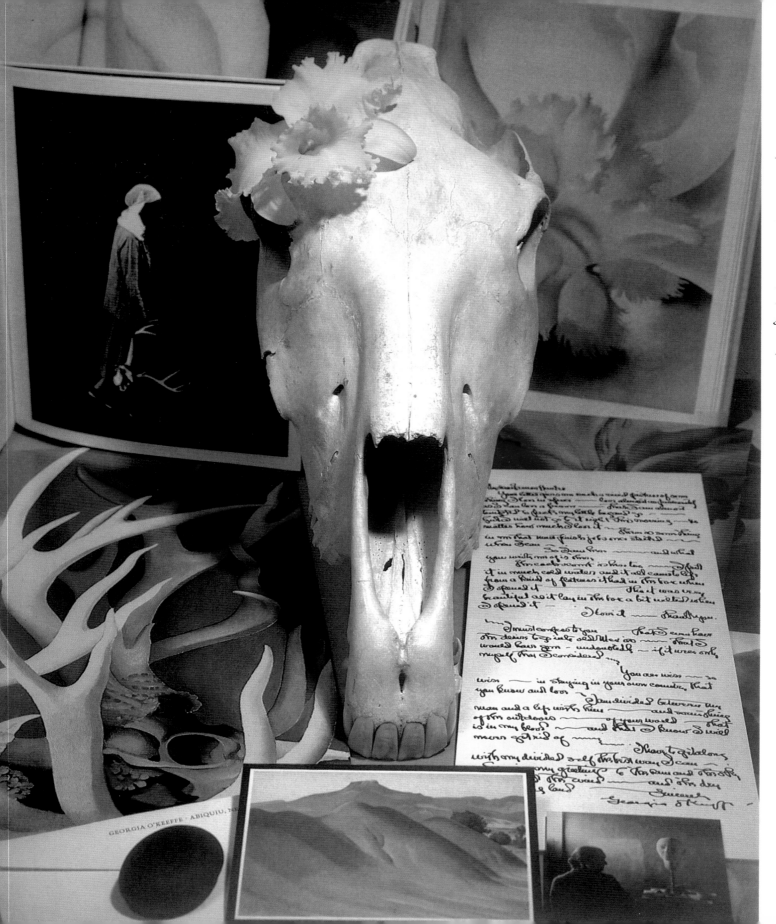

Georgia O'Keeffe, 1988

Using the giant Polaroid camera in the Massachusetts College of Art, Kalman has paid homage to many artists he admires. Here he remembers Georgia O'Keeffe with a black smooth stone (such as one from her collection), her painting of the pedernal in Abiquiu, a set of antlers and photographic portraits of her by Todd Webb and Eliot Porter.

Gyorgy Kepes, 1988

In honor of his friend, the artist Gyuri Kepes, Kalman arranged the painter's palette, one of his paintings, a birthday gift, card, and a snapshot of the two of them critiquing photographs. No ordinary still life would do, for we have here an example of the "new vision" photography that Kepes espoused, an arrangement that moves beyond two-dimensional formalism into the illusion of choreographed space.

55

**International Balloon Festival,
Albuquerque, NM, 1982**

*A close look suggests that these
brightly colored marbles on the
sand are balloons about to take off.*

Early Ascension, 1982

*Each year the balloon festival kicks off
at sunrise with a dramatic mass ascension.
Because the early morning air is cool,
the hot air balloons rise quickly.*

**Storm Over the Organ
Mountains, White Sands,
NM, 1985**

*Although Béla's Southwest land-
scapes recall color field paintings,
he provides evidence of the world's
own magic metamorphoses.*

Chiaroscuro, 1980

*God's art director enlisted
mineral seepage
to provide the interplay
of light and dark on the walls of
Canyon de Chelly in Arizona.*

*State Folk Dance Assemblage,
Budapest, 1983*

Redwood slices, California, 1985
Throughout his career, Bèla has
loved rhythmically repeated patterns.

55 YEARS OF PHOTOGRAPHY

Béla Kalman's life-long creativity as an independent photographic artist and as a commercial photographer has produced a remarkable diversity of imagery: timeless black and white views of a sculptor's studio or a museum interior made in his native Hungary in the early 1950s co-exist with psychedelically-colored pictorial fantasies produced in the heady atmosphere of the liberated sixties. His sympathetic portraits of visual artists he reveres such as the great Japanese woodcut master Munakata or his friend the Hungarian-born painter and experimental photographer Gyorgy Kepes reveal his human empathy as well as his visual sensitivity. His many images that play variations on the organic shapes of leaves and flowers display great elegance of form: Mother Nature as the most sophisticated and innovative of modern designers. ■ An exceptionally poetic example from among his numerous still-life arrangements, many produced for advertising, is the photograph that places the juicy reds of freshly cut pomegranates against the cool purity of a white porcelain plaque that has a relief design portraying the ancient Pompeian motif of the merchandizing of little Loves or Cupids. ■ One of the recurrent themes of twentieth-century photography is the rediscovery or reappraisal of work that was originally produced primarily for commercial reasons: fashion, illustration, advertising. Béla's work is an excellent example of the vitality that can result from the intertwining of commercially driven inventiveness and independent artistic motives. ■ A unifying thread which unites many categories of Béla's images is his obsessive love of rhythmically repeated patterns: the tubular forms of Parisian chimney pots and roof tiles or ovals and circles of stacked automobile mufflers—black and white images that have the lively optical vibration of the paintings and prints of Kalman's countryman Victor Vasarely. The sequencing of this book is full of juxtapositions in which Béla makes pictures captured at different times and places speak to each other, underscoring his preoccupation with pattern and with the visual pun. ■ When he turned to color in the early sixties Kalman experimented with a high-key abstract color: for example, a pair of mandala-like images in which the image of a nude female model seated in a lotus position is multiplied by a trick plastic lens until it resembles a sheet of postage stamps. Béla once characteristically asked me while planning the layout of an exhibition—moving reduced-scale black and white prints about on a table top—if I thought an image of whirling Hungarian folk dancers with balooning skirts should be hung next to a photograph of an outdoor display of slab tables made from cross-sections of California redwood trees. This lively interplay of visually punning patterns was wonderfully revealing of Béla's witty, playful side, an essential aspect of his photographic vision.

Clifford S. Ackley, Curator
Prints, Drawings & Photographs
Museum of Fine Arts, Boston
October, 1993

Butterfly Maidens and Koshare Clowns, Galisteo, NM, 1989

Having developed his eye as a theater and ballet photographer in Hungary, Kalman regards all the world as a stage. He often focuses on the exotic choreography and costumes seen at Indian dances.

Eagle Dancer, Santa Clara Pueblo, NM, 1986

*Photographing eagle dancers, Béla
honors the high-flying, far-seeing
vision of eagles. Surely they
are his spirit animals.*

The Dissident, 1990

Though art critics protest Santa
Fe's ubiquitous howling coyotes, few
howl as doggedly as this lone dissi-
dent at Jackalope's.

Elaine's Men, 1992
Legendary Santa Fe art dealer
Elaine Horwitch protected her
premises with a lineup of trigger-
happy gunslingers.

Dancing Apsaras, 1970

These celestial dancers carved on a sandstone pillar at Angkor were probably modeled after court dancers who entertained the Khmer King Jayavarman VII back in the thirteenth century.

Cambodian Royal Dancers, 1970

Classical dancers in Cambodia and Thailand continue the dance traditions carved into the stones at Angkor nearly a thousand years ago. Here members of a troop wear traditional silk and gold lamé garments.

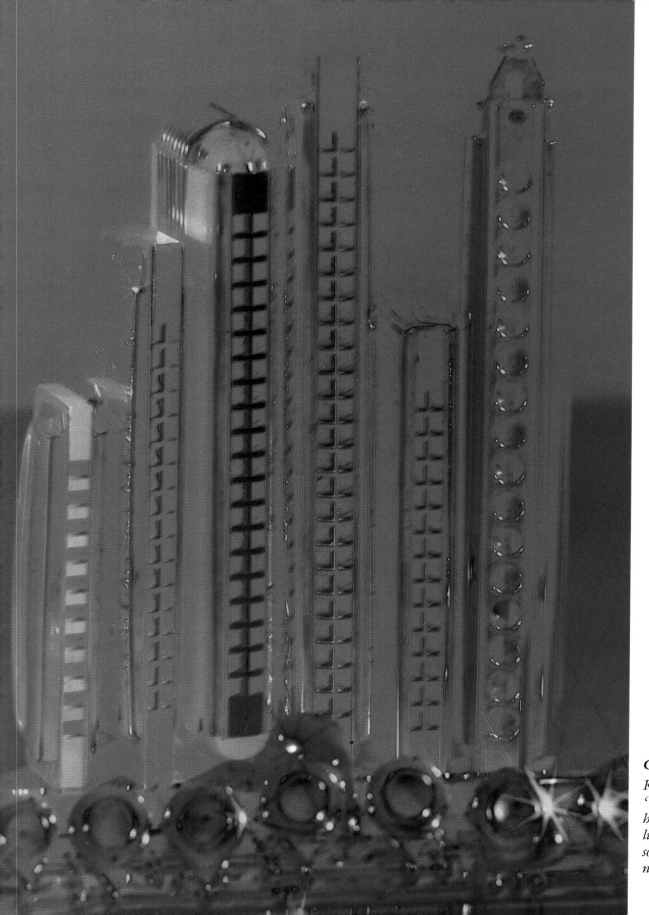

Cityscape, 1979
Kalman played the
"Wizard of Aahs" when
he transformed these modest
little harmonicas (through
solarization) into a jazzy,
neon cityscape.

68

Solarized Flutes, 1979

To hit the right note, Béla solarized these flutes. His innovative process involved interrupting the development of the color negatives, relighting them with colored gel covered lights, then continuing with the newly introduced colors.

Solarized Tuba, 1979
This brass band instrument is transformed into abstract colorful shapes and forms and booms to a very bright beat!

Country Wedding Musicians, 1992

*Viewers can almost hear the ooom
pah pah of the sousaphones and
the beat of the drums at this
old-fashioned country wedding
in Oaxaca, Mexico.*

Entrance to Angkor Wat, 1970

In 1970 the Kalmans traveled to Cambodia to visit the great stone monuments of Angkor, which were built by a series of Khmer kings from the ninth to the thirteenth centuries. The intricate sandstone carvings depict themes common to the Hindu and Buddhist faiths.

Early Mondrian, 1970

The simple rectangular purity of this red barn in Lincoln, Massachusetts, reminded Kalman of works by the Dutch artist Piet Mondrian.

American Pavilion, Montreal Expo 1967

The publicity photo of Marilyn Monroe, the painted illustrations of NASA's parachutes and Buckminster Fuller's geodesic dome play off one another like elements in a collage. Visual non-sequiturs occur whenever the different idioms of representation coincide. Kalman makes the most of this, bidding viewers to play the "what is it?" game.

American Pavilion, 1967

Actress Carol Lombard and a New York City taxicab appear realer than real in this rowdy, pop art-like photograph taken at the Montreal Expo in 1967.

Ugly House, Tel Aviv, 1986

So similar, so different! Kalman calls the oozing, flaking building at left "the ugliest house I have ever seen." The pockmarked cliff dwellings at right, however, are ancient, ingenious storage vaults for wine and fruit.

76

Cliff Dwellings in Cappadocia,
Turkey, 1992

High Power Summit, 1989

*Kalman spoofs self-important
political summits in which the
participants invariably cross their
wires. Here four telephone men
engage in small talk.*

Sidestreet towards the Duomo, 1988

Pedestrians and motorists alike find it's a tight squeeze in Florence, Italy. What captivated the photographer was the over-hanging roofs—architectural umbrellas useful for anyone caught in the rain.

**Theater Facade,
Munich, Germany,
1991**

*It may be a distinguished old landmark
theater, but in Kalman's photograph
its double pediment looks tiny, toylike
and a bit silly.*

Cupola, 1990

*This one-of-a-kind chess set
is in fact a detail from Tucson's
Xavier del Bac Mission Church.*

Guggenheim's Calder, 1993
*Using his ''third eye'' Kalman held
the camera over his head and
snapped the shutter. Though this
mobile captured in a still
photograph becomes, in effect,
a Calder stabile, the scarlet
discs continue to transform the
surrounding space because of the
sculptor's vigorous, open design.*

Lunch is Served,
Ventana Canyon Hotel,
Tucson, AZ, 1990

May Day, Paris, 1992

The tricolored French national flag curtains the heroic gate, increasing our suspense as we await a patriotic drama to unfold.

New Entrance to the Louvre, Paris, 1989

Visitors to the Louvre enter the future through I.M. Pei's galactic pyramid only to move full speed backwards into the mists of art history.

Abandoned Mineshaft near Creede, Colorado, 1985

More important than the character and curiosity value of this abandoned 19th century mineshaft is the way it sums up the ongoing collision between the forces of development versus preservation and free enterprise versus regulation in the American West.

Storage Tanks, Big Island, Hawaii, 1988

How many people look long and hard at storage tanks? Taking a worm's eye view, Kalman found stunning geometries and striking patterns of light and shadow.

Storage Silo, Hawaii, 1988
Photographing the gentle geometry
of this simple silo, Kalman
found a new way to convey
the pastoral ideal.

Grand Tetons, Wyoming, 1985

*The ink-blue mountains combined
with their reflections in the
lake become an all-natural
Rorschach test.*

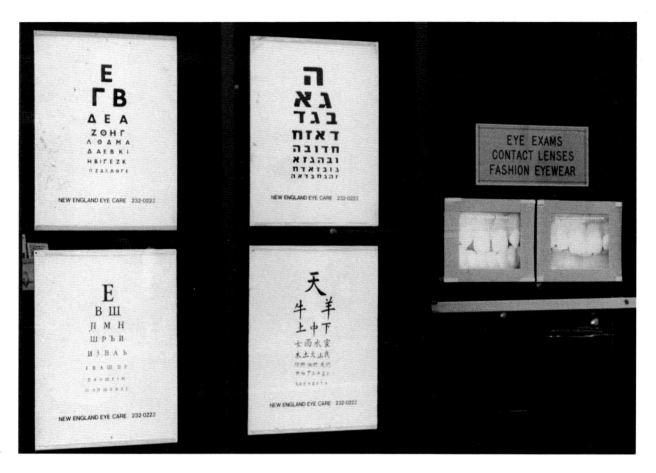

Eye Tester, Brighton, MA, 1980
Kalman knew he'd found a subject to bite into when he spied this odd combination of foreign eye charts and local dental pictures.

VISUAL VENTURES

Béla Kalman's photographs are a meld of history, art and cultural investigations. He gets on film all kinds of subjects as he travels over the world giving us armchair tourists a sense of intimacy with places and people we may never see firsthand. His photographs provide us with glimpses of ordinary life in rural and urban areas as well as bring us up close to majestic historical monuments as well as nature in its most dramatic moods. As an artist he shares with us his delight when he encounters patches of brilliant colors or details denoting the passage of time or evidence of work created by the skilled hands of a craftsman. ■ Notable is the formal consistency of his pictures. Sometimes the consistency does not come across at first for it is beneath the surface of his photographs. This underpinning of shapes and colors turn his richly informative photographs into images we come back to or linger over for a second and third look.
■ Kalman responds to and registers on film details one might overlook even if walking beside him but as he moves to the left or right to better frame an image or isolates a subject from completing elements he reveals a new world to us that is part fiction, part fact. He often decontextualizes a subject by eliminating scale references, thereby creating images that are quite independent of what was in front of his camera. ■ Kalman gives us lessons about how to get more from a photograph. He believes he can engender by the close juxtaposition of two images ideas that would not so readily be apparent if only a single photograph were being viewed. From his two picture formulations emerge meanings more far reaching than if he depended on a single image. Some of his linked photographs require very close scrutiny to make them convey

his concepts—others have obvious common traits that through symbiotic relationships evoke a smile or an involuntary movement of the head up and down as we "see" what he has created. The effects Kalman achieves result from his sensitivity to solutions of structural problems that nature has solved eons ago and man now uses in design and architecture. There is a ripple effect when we learn how to study the combinations in this book. Our perceptions are sharpened and our curiosity aroused when we see next to each other a wall full of petroglyphs from the American Southwest across from a wall of eye examination cards which have been printed with blocks of letters in four different languages ranging from Chinese to Hebrew, which impresses us with the differences and similarities between what nature and man have created. ▇ In Kalman's work aesthetic qualities concentrate our responses as unexpected similarities echo from one picture to another. Well represented in this challenging game is the picture of the steel corrugated roof with vents sticking out of the top of an industrial or large farm building placed alongside one of his pictures of a serrated top of the world encrusted in snow and mirrored in a glassy lake. Initially these two photographs seem uneasily matched one with the other but if we study the two we find connections. This, like reading evidence in a well-written detective story, is what he intends. We eventually understand that the pictures complement each other and thereby make a strong case for relating them. Our powers of observation and imagination are sharpened as Kalman rhymes and parallels the extremely varied collection of photographs found illustrated in The Third Eye.

Van Deren Coke
Santa Fe, New Mexico
September, 1993

Newspaper Rock, 1993
Kalman calls this "newspaper rock" near Monticello, Utah, an "eyetester." The inscriptions were made hundreds of years ago by the Ute Indians.

Misty Night, 1991

Kalman was awed by the sheer size of New York City's skyscrapers when he first arrived in America and he still looks for fresh, new ways to convey their staggering proportions. Here darkness purified the scene and eliminated daytime clutter, while a 20mm lens helped the photographer mime the nightlife he perceived in these giddily, leaning buildings.

Tsarskoye Selo,
St. Petersburg, 1970
All that glitters is gold
in this chapel built
by the czar with
the Midas touch.

The Quiet Sea at Acapulco, 1971

A single silhouetted sailboat on the water prevents this photograph from joining the realm of pure abstraction. It is a rare noon in Acapulco when many sailboats aren't crisscrossing the sea.

Sunset in Rio, 1992

Tiny details often change the meaning of Kalman's photographs. Here a cross on the mountain summit competes with scores of power stations needed to provide the electricity for the millions who live in Rio de Janeiro. The pastoral ideal is clearly under technological enroachment and God might be losing ground to Mammon.

Western Wall, Jerusalem, Israel, 1986
Kalman photographed these
two sacred places at Easter,
the first teeming with
praying orthodox Jews,
the second crowded with
Christian pilgrims.

Via Dolorosa, Jerusalem, 1986

97

Yellowstone Geyser, 1985

*Awed by the explosive energy
of this geyser, Kalman
thought of "the Big
Bang at the beginning
of creation."*

Na Pali Coast, Kauai, Hawaii, 1988
Kalman hastens to tell you that
this is not a trick photograph.
Rainbows in Kauai often appear
below helicopters.

Fall Scene, Hyde Park Road, Santa Fe, 1987

This forest of sun-kissed aspens inspired a local painter who in turn inspired Kalman. He has long loved pictures within pictures.

George Segal's Sculpture in Brookline, MA, 1987

Back in the 1960s Pop artist George Segal gained a reputation for spookily eloquent white plaster figures which he placed in real, everyday settings. Here Kalman moves a step further, photographing the works transformed yet again with a layer of snow.

Early Snowfall, 1983

He has traveled all over the world, yet Kalman—like his fellow Hungarian André Kertész—has made many of his best photographs right out of his front window.

Melting Snow, Santa Fe, NM, 1992
*During the winter icy stalactites
regularly appear in the historic
gallery district of Canyon Road.*

Barnstable, Cape Cod, 1983

The sight of this bewigged tombstone would surely make Edward Gorey shiver with delight.

Memorial Day, Cape Cod, 1983

When the American flag blows
in the wind, its stars and
stripes become ghostly tempests
of red, white and blue.

**Carousel Horse,
Oaxaca, Mexico, 1992**

*The painters and carvers of
carousel horses have long worked
under the aesthetic premise
that "too much is not enough."
Accordingly, Kalman's photograph
explodes with garish color,
ricocheting space, and hyped
up energy.*

City Flags
Siena, Italy, 1988

Béla played the part of Prince
of Prints and Sultan of Silks
when he photographed
these flags in Siena.

Sailboats on the Charles River, Boston, 1983

Railroad Yard, Brighton, MA, 1983

*In the 1960s Kalman's love of gestural
sweep and swirl led him to choreograph
space. "In 1983 a moving still photo was
an enigma," says the photographer, who
acquired his first zoom lens that year. To
create the effect of motion in these two
photographs, he put his camera on a tripod,
closed the lens down to the smallest opening
and made a five to ten second exposure as he
zoomed the lens from one end to the other.*

**Henry Moore Sculpture,
Brookline, MA, 1987**

*Henry Moore's sculptures—
known for weight, permanence
and grandeur—seem
elusive, even a bit eerie,
when transformed by snow
and shadow.*

110

Allan Houser, Galisteo, NM, 1985

"As old as I am, I am excited to come to work every day," says the 80 year old sculptor Allan Houser. Known throughout the world as the patriarch of Native American Sculptors, he refuses to rest on past achievements and says he is constantly "searching for new hunting grounds." At 72 Kalman shares that goal.

Graffiti in Brighton, MA, 1983

*Many modern artists see the freedom
of primitive art in the immediate
techniques and fragmented
symbols of graffiti.*
*Speeding in and out with his zoom
lens, Kalman used the latest in
photo technology to produce ghostly
figures that could have come
from any era and civilization.*

Outdoor Sculpture, Early Snow in Brookline, MA, 1987

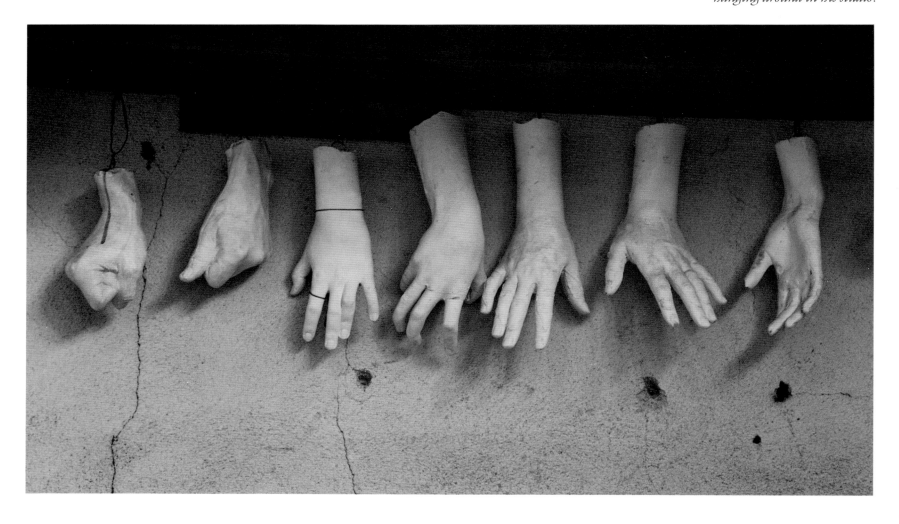

World's Largest Palette, 1987

*Ever entranced with the biggest
and best, Béla found this
Brobdingnagian painter's palette
at the Palm Springs Desert
Museum in California. "It has a
colorful but slightly confused
message about what art is,"
says the photographer with a big laugh.*

BÉLA'S FIELD OF DREAMS

Béla Kalman arrived in America in 1956 with a suitcase packed with a shaving kit, plenty of innocence and his proverbial third eye. Leaving Hungary behind, he gained something he had not truly enjoyed since childhood; the chance to be instinctive and impulsive. These qualities would revitalize his photographic career. ■ He responded quickly to the mind-boggling, eye-popping mass of consumer goods available in America. Like a kid in a toy shop, he was entranced by the unending bright colors, bold contrasts and lively surprises. Limited for years by the dreary scarcity of goods in wartime and Communist Hungary, he regarded this brand new capitalist world with open, expansive appreciation. His genuine regard for the consumer wonderland would within a decade make Kalman a name to remember in advertising photography. ■ As soon as he settled in, he began learning about artistic and technical developments in art and photography, adapting nearly everything to his own aesthetic. Ever the experimenter, he bedazzled viewers with pyrotechnics and ingenious improvisations. ■ Like many modernists, Kalman sought to liberate photography from its point of reference. Amplifying and sometimes totally altering on-the-site impressions, he makes them bigger, brighter, and better. He particularly loved the transformative power of solarization, turning tubas and other silver and brass musical instruments into syncopated near abstractions or even into "mini cities" pulsating to a booming red and green beat. Giant closeups of flowers burst with life's buzzing, blooming confusion.

Madonna and Child, Onion Slice, 1971

■ Out of the studio, his lens registered moving trains and cars as dynamic calligraphic streaks. Playing with peculiarly photographic distortions he let tall buildings lean back rakishly, their massive forms seemingly perforated by night. Straightforward portrayals of skyscrapers, steel cables and other evidence of advanced technology would never have aroused the diverse and conflicting sensations that Kalman compressed into his semi-abstract compositions. He would have us sense the flash and flicker of lights, the vertigo of high places, the frenzied flow of moving traffic, the hustle and bustle of city life. Most of all, he wants us to dance along with him to the snapping rhythms of American life. ■ Kalman's love of movement is also seen in his many photographs of Alexander Calder's mobiles swooping, trembling, gliding and cutting dynamic paths through real, not simulated space. The photographer shares this sculptor's fascination with motion and space, and like him tends to avoid that which is staid or **116** static. Like sculptor Henry Moore, Kalman loves vacuums that are, paradoxically, as important as form itself and composite images in which one form is suggestively contained within another. The photographer, too, enjoys making what is — seem to be what it is not, a widespread habit among modern artists who often prefer ambiguity to fact. ▨ The games continue with hidden surprises. Tiny details give viewers the unexpected thrill of finding a provocative connection or visual joke. A baby cross perched on a larger cross, a mini sculpture on a large one. A theater in Munich with double pediments, one painted, one sculpted, becomes a gewgawed toy set or a game about context, facade and illusion. "Light bulbs light up when you see something and feel you can do something with it," he says with a prankster's grin. ▨ Often Kalman imagines the improbable and impossible: the incredible (non) edible of a opal in an avocado, tulips flaunting parrotlike plumage and a cut onion that resembles a madonna and child. (One thinks of the faithful who see Madonnas on tortillas, though this photographer is more magician than mystic.) Most often such observations are witty: witness his rebuttal of Pablo Picasso's twisted, rotated faces, "Picasso's a bad boy spoiling God's creation," comments Kalman.) ▨ In such works, he takes the capital A out of art. He rejects old-fashioned theories that hold that only permanent, valuable or respected materials are prerequisites for esthetic delight. Kalman would be loose, free and spontaneous, and make photographs that are generous, playful and ecumenical. A boyish man of voracious visual appetites, he rejects criticism to say, "Look at this, and this and this." ▨ Although he knew the terror of Hitler's mass rallies, Kalman prefers satire to protest. He remembers how in 1936 his fellow Hungarian Stefan Lorant, the pioneering editor of the *Munchner Illustrierte Presse* and later the English magazine *Lilliput*, showed a picture of Hitler "barking" beside a photograph of Einstein giving him the raspberry. Kalman too is guided by the keen perception that viewers wish to laugh as well as think. Spotting a "mass rally" of folk art coyotes at Jackalope's in Santa Fe, he noted the lone dissident howling to the beat of a different drummer. Similarly, he replaced the frightening lines of real life armed soldiers of his memory with carved gunslinging cowboys. Whereas other photographers approaching this subject matter might be denouncing America's runaway perils of consumerism and kitsch, Kalman finds the subject ripe for a long and hearty laugh. No longer in a country where contradictory directions or messages constitute a life and death matter, he can chuckle at the visual joke of road signs pointing in opposite directions. Rarely if ever does he get caught at a crossroads. Taking the route most traveled on one day, he explores the least traveled the next. Both widen his horizons; failures are merely detours on the path to success. ▨ In recent years he has traveled to Cambodia, Brazil, France, Israel, Italy and other countries to sample the world's wonders. Still, America—with its emphasis on exaggeration, on youth and on too much, too fast, too soon—remains Béla Kalman's field of dreams.

Picasso's Onion, 1971

Sally Eauclaire,
Santa Fe, October 1993

117

Two Lincolns, in Daniel Chester French's Studio, Stockbridge, MA, 1986

Great men—including Abe Lincoln—come in all sizes.

**Church Detail near Tajique,
New Mexico, 1985**

*Christian missionaries everywhere
hope that mother crosses will
spawn lots of baby crosses.*

*Entrance to the
National Gallery, 1990*

Visiting the National Gallery
in Washington, D.C. Kalman
photographed an angular
sculpture at the entrance from
a low angle that makes it
appear bizarrely blockaded and
strangely inaccessible. Then
again maybe the photographer is
speculating on what a Mondrian
exhibition would look like after
an earthquake or if taken apart
to be reconstituted as a Rubik cube.

120/121

**Wind Generated Energy, near
Palm Springs, California, 1987**

This pinwheel wonderland provides
cheap wind-generated power.

Jerusalem and a Calder Mobile, 1986

*Is that the world's brightest,
biggest bug or a fantastic new
Rube Goldberg device? Using a
telephoto lens, Kalman dramatical-
ly compressed the space in order
to bring Alexander Calder's
sculpture and a newly built
suburb together.*

Old Town Dubrovnik, 1978

*The 500-year old town of Dubrovnik
was nearly destroyed in 1991.
Most of the ancient buildings
jumbled together on the hillside in
this picture are now history.*

Uranium Mine Pit near Grants, New Mexico, 1984
The brightly colored, mosaic-like patches are effluent
holding ponds in which liquid waste products evaporate
until they are solid enough to be taken away and dumped.

White Sands National Monument, Summer Storm
near the Organ Mountains, NM, 1984
Peaceful and holy as this scene appears, it's only
a hop and skip away from missile testing grounds.

"Stargazer," 1987
Lipstick, party favor, rocket? At this San Diego sculpture site Alexander Lieberman's work is quite the vogue.

Magic Tree near Cochiti, 1985
Of this spooky scene, Kalman jokes "I posed the sun to make the magic."

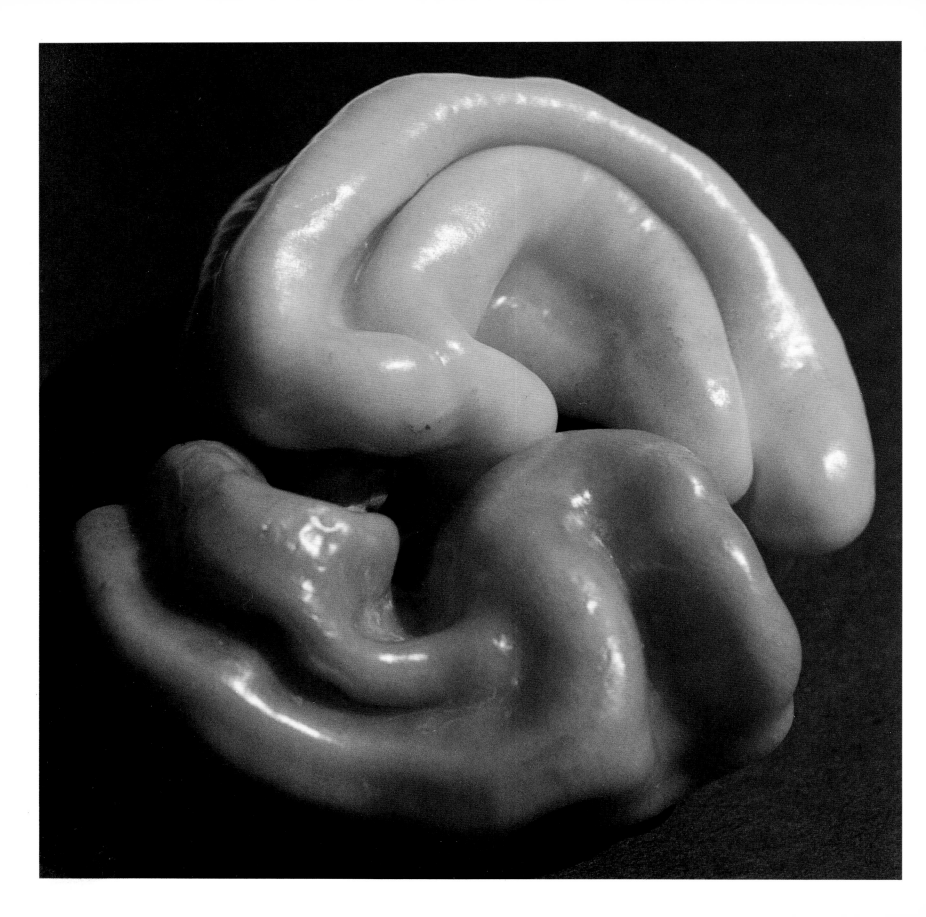

**Yin Yang in the
Green Pepper World,
Cape Cod, 1984**

The sensuous curves of these
peppers could represent lovers
embracing, twins in utero or
the concept of yin/yang. Like
photographer Edward Weston,
Kalman relishes perfect form.

Cactus in Bloom, 1989

Why go bushwhacking in the
jungle when exotic floral
specimens exist right
at home? He found this
flowering cactus near La Tierra
Nueva, north of Santa Fe.

Pomegranate Still Life, Boston, 1973

The pomegranate's blood-red juice and many seeds have made it a symbol of eternity and fertility since ancient times. Its crownlike terminal makes it the fruit of royalty. In this studio still life made for a greeting card company, Kalman contrasts the life-giving fruit with pure white sculptural reliefs of prankish cupids and other gods and goddesses well versed in the ways of love.

Spices, Boston, 1961

This mellow and patinaed studio setup for an S.S. Pierce Company advertisement made customers think of old-fashioned quality control. The spices appear so freshly ground that we can nearly smell their fragrant aromas.

OVERLEAF:
French Tulip, 1990

This French tulip bursts with energy and crackles with visual surprise.

Poppy, 1992

Kalman found this bright orange poppy in Santa Fe painter Ford Ruthling's backyard.

Calla Triangle, Boston, 1990

Georgia's Calla, Cape Cod, 1989
*Kalman calls calla lilies "the
most photogenic flowers.
They are every photographer's
great inspiration."*

The ancient stones of these
buildings provide a neutral
ground against which the saturated
colors of the laundry can pop and glow.

Baja Boatyard, *1979*

*Kalman couldn't resist making
an abstraction out of the patches
of coruscating colors provided
by the pleasure vessels docked at
Baja's Smallcraft Harbor
in Southern Hungary.*

***A Violent Summer Storm,
Santa Fe, NM 1985***

*At heart Kalman is a sensualist,
seduced by the pleasures of
seeing. Photographing at dusk,
when the strident contrasts of
midday light dissolve into soft,
subtly nuanced hues, he can
savor delicate, unexpected color
shifts. He sighted this fan
shaped fantasy just before sunset,
right after a storm.*

Walking Rain, Santa Fe, 1987

*The title refers to a
phenomenon of the south-
west, wherein a hiker can
walk out of the rain into
an area that is sunny and dry.*

Cooling Mechanism,
Polaroid Plant,
Cambridge, MA, 1989

Kalman passionately loves the clear,
clean machines and engineering
found in America, where the latest
buildings sometimes look like
they've been turned inside out.

Church Entrance, Picuris Pueblo, NM, 1982
Kalman often sees pictures within
pictures at the old southwestern mission churches.

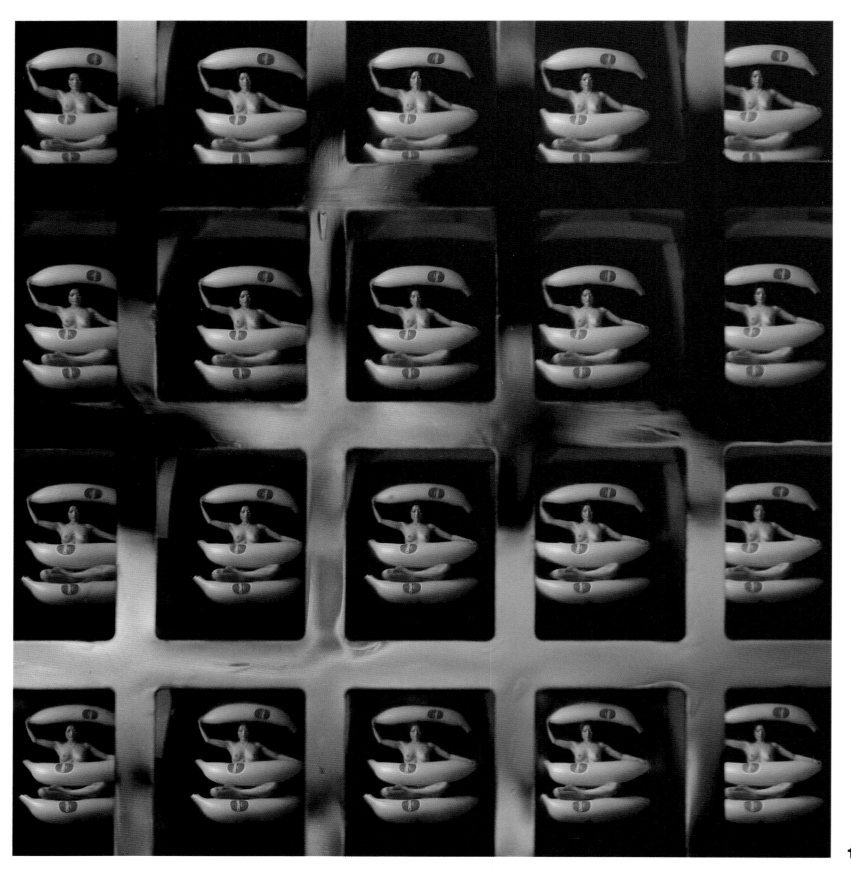

***Chiquita Banana
Fantasy,
Boston, MA, 1968***

*In the heady atmo-
sphere of the 1960s
Kalman became a
master purveyor of pop,
op, camp and corn.
Here he used a Fresnel
lens to photograph a
yogi-like model sand-
wiched between
banana-shaped bal-
loons. Although the
"top bananas" at
Chiquita declined to
use this bumble-bee
colored McYogi burger
in their advertising
campaign, the pho-
tographer has long
considered it one of his
funkiest and most
puzzling photos.*

***Banana Blossoms
and Fruit, 1969***

*On assignment for the
United Fruit Company in
San Pedro Sula, Honduras,
Kalman discovered a
powerful image of lust
and fertility.*

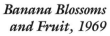

143

Blackbirds, the Everglades, Florida, 1989

There aren't four and twenty blackbirds here and the swampland is no poultry pie, yet this photograph has a lurid, gothic quality that's not too far removed from the nursery rhyme.

Elegant Orchid, Boston, MA, 1983

Working for a greeting card company, he produced an exotic effect by placing colored gels in front of his strobe lights.

Dolmabagci, Istanbul, Turkey, 1992

*Coming out of darkness, that
metaphor for blindness, the view
appears more brilliant, more
true than ever before.*

Cabo San Lucas, Mexico, 1990
Even nature celebrates The
Day of the Dead in Mexico.

Napa Landscape, California, 1992

*Rather than fall prey to picturesque cliches, Kalman tried a new
format in which two views of the Napa Valley seem "reflected" on
the "lenses" of a pair of giant "eyeglasses."*

Bridal Veil Falls, 1994

Every visitor is inspired by Yosemite National Park; Ansel Adams made it every photographer's challenge.

Atomic Winter, Photogram, 1983

Despite the wild, "mutated" colors, essential energy continues to course through all things, including the veins of this leaf.

Red Buoys, Chatham, MA, 1987

Bumping against each other, these lobster buoys coalesced into a field of flat, pure red. The view through the "peephole" helps viewers play the "What is it?" game.

**Botero on Park Avenue,
New York City, 1993**

Fernando Botero's brawny body-
builder joins the ranks of ancient
Greek and Roman statuary; he has
lost his head, arms and legs but
retained that all-important
little fig leaf.

Mormon Church, La Jolla, CA, 1993

*Béla made this cubist photograph under the midday sun,
the only time of day when bright light and black shadows
would fragment and multiply this church's spiky spires.*

Christmas in San Diego, 1994
*Horton Plaza's giddy jumble of colors, patterns
shapes and textures—including funky shops
cut like a wedge of cheese—makes childlike
visitors and photographers clap with joy.*

Boston South Station Post Office aircontrol ducts, MA, 1987

The oddly shaped ducts bring the cool harbor air in, but that doesn't help to move the mail any faster.

La Jolla Boogie Woogie, 1994
Electronic imagery is this photographer's
latest passion. Who can say what's next?

Ford's Poppy according to the Gospel of Andy Warhol, 1994
What colors nature hasn't invented, the photographer can.

The Cove, La Jolla, CA, 1993

*This swinging tree deserved
a proper dance partner—
Béla's shadow.*

158

stopped. "Only the desperados read in bed. I was one of them." His drawing talent manifested at age nine at summer camp run by a child psychiatrist trained in the Montessori system. When he illustrated the camp's magazine, his father predicted a great future for him in the communication field. ■ As a boy scout, Béla passed a battery of tests: tying knots, throwing a boomerang, roping cattle ("we practiced by lassoing each other"), communicating by Morse Code, starting a camp fire, pitching a tent, and identifying minerals, animals, insects and birds. He was especially clever at observing objects and writing them down from memory. ■ In 1933, young Kalman qualified for the World Scout Jamboree held in Godollo, a small town east of Budapest, and served in the honor guard of Sir Baden Powell. "He was like God," he remembers. "He was about 80 years old. To see him and even have him talk to us! That was sheer heaven." ■ By age 13, Kalman grew interested in the outside world. He followed Mussolini's Ethiopian war, Hitler's annexation of the Saar region and Hungarian politics. Mostly, 1936 was the year of the Olympics. "All of us were glued to our radios." ■ Kalman knew several Olympic wrestlers because they had practiced at Fodor Sport Camp, which he had attended that summer. "Wrestling teacher Karoly Karpati tic-tac-toed his opponents in seconds," he says. "After five bouts, there he was on the high stand receiving his gold medal in his red bathing suit-like wrestling outfit with the Royal Hungarian Coat of Arms emblazoned on his pants. I told everyone that an Olympic champion practiced on me." Meanwhile, his own sporting abilities were improving. By 1937, he could run 100 meters in eleven seconds. ■ The next summer, he worked as golf caddy at the Hungarian Golf Club. "Participants sounded like a roll call of the Hungarian aristocracy, Prince this, Count that, Baron so and so, all with hyphenated names, all ancient Austro-Hungarian feudalists. So I was very disappointed when I was called to be the auxiliary caddy for a guy with a plain name: Bobby Jones. Today when I lick the back of the U.S. stamp depicting the leading golf champion of this country, I have to smile." ■ The "kicsi" was not an academic superachiever. In the fall of 1936 his parents hired a tutor to help him with chemistry, botany, math, physics, Latin and Italian. She taught Béla how to be organized, how to approach a subject and how to fathom the essence of each assignment, skills that would later aid his career in photography. "But at that time I was not happy to be coached and was ashamed that I couldn't manage my work by myself." Kalman never did well in German. His mother understood, saying, "Can you blame him after all the barking Hitler does on the radio about the international Jewish conspiracy?" ■ Béla remembers the Berzsenyi Gymnasium building well. Built in 1858 of brick and stone, its main hall (where oral and written exams took place) had a 50 foot ceiling, 20 foot windows and 20 foot oil paintings of Greek and Roman mythological scenes. "We lived in great fear, as if our lives depended on our grades and for some of us it did." ■ "Only the As were accepted at universities. One B and you couldn't even apply. This was, of course, the rule for the

Béla on his tricycle, 1926

Boy Scout, 1934

This 1925 group portrait shows Béla's relatives dressed in the height of fashion.

Jews. The gentiles had no problem. For us, our grades were vital. If at university, you couldn't be drafted. So we studied very hard."
■ Hungarian history involved a thousand years of names and dates of reigns, laws, conquests. Literature meant 200 writers and poets, and being able to quote from memory. "Fifty years later, they are still in my 'computer.' I can recite them at any time." ■ Unlike his brother Pista, who had earned all As and gone on to law school, Béla "flunked" out with one A, two Bs and 3Cs. In the anti-semitic quota system of the late thirties and forties, college was not a possibility unless he went abroad.
■ Béla would have studied at Columbia University in New York City had

The "four leaf clover" family in 1935.

Hitler not invaded Poland, causing the outbreak of World War II. Shortly after, Kalman's father got a call from the U.S. Consulate saying that his son's visa was suspended because of the hostile activities in Germany and its ally Hungary. ■ Kalman had aspired to be a journalist ever since his father had published an article by him about the Concours d'Elegance, a classy parade of the latest foreign cars. This success at age 16 drove him to improve his vocabulary and style by studying works by Cervantes, Racine, Dumas, Zola, Garcia Lorca, and other writers and poets. ■ When his visa didn't arrive, Kalman had to change his career plans—and fast. Photography was chosen by his family. "Those three muses, my parents and my brother were in full control of me. Their advice was law. I was not a rebellious child and I listened carefully when they decided what 'the little one' should do for a career."
■ Photography was first recommended by a career testing firm named Indorg (an abbreviation for Industrial Organization). In 1938, after spending several days in their office, the verdict came in: Béla was a good observer, firm decision maker, quick executor, poor color selector and not musical. They recommended handicraft work requiring manual skill such as photography, dairy farming, pottery or gardening. Uncle Gyula, a skilled amateur photographer who earned extra money photographing fixtures for a lightbulb manufacturer, also endorsed the idea. ■ Béla agreed: "I had an artistic bent and this sounded feasible. I knew I couldn't sit on my tushie for 48 hours a week. I needed to move around, make individual decisions and judgments." ■ Kalman first apprenticed with one of his father's friends, Francis Szantho, a press representative of Reuter and Havas News Agencies in Budapest. For a fee, he learned how to develop, load holders and use Leicas. Within two days he was on location, helping make ID photos of factory employees. Back in the studio, he copied 8×10 inch glossies, including a rooftop photograph of a crowd in Berlin screaming "Heil Hitler" as the Fuehrer announced that his troops had marched into Poland. ■ Though Kalman's talents pleased Szantho, the master's mother—"the most beaked owl looking lady I have ever seen"—fired him for cleaning a parquet floor by spraying water in figure eights. "What did I know about proper cleaning?" ■ Kalman soon moved on to an apprenticeship with a born-

again Christian named Geza Borsody, who kept him busy retouching, hand coloring prints and playing a record of Ravel's *Bolero* for the studio's parakeets. Once a week, he went to trade school to learn about lenses, cameras, optics and the history of photography. ■ In the summer of 1940, Kalman passed his apprentice exam and was hired as a retoucher by Dezso Rozgonyi, "an overweight, arthritic, heavy breather with a Franz Liszt hairdo." Pay was the streetcars' fare. Hours were 7:30 a.m. to 7 p.m. or later, six days a week. ■ The next spring Kalman became "a very happy fellow" at the Varkonyi Studio, where he learned the subtleties of fine printing and was even paid for it. László Varkonyi, whom

Graduation portrait, age 18.

Graduating class, Berzsenyi Gimnasium, 1939

he remembers as "a mumbler except when he growled like a gorilla," painstakingly went over every print he made. "At first, he tore up half of my work. After that, almost none." ■ The clientele was made up of the aristocracy, untitled nobility and theater people. Portraits were heavily retouched. "People wanted to look slim. Wrinkles, blemishes, hair loss and double chins were not in vogue so half of our crew kept busy eliminating these problems. If the person still resembled himself, it was a successful portrait." ■ When Varkonyi was drafted into a Jewish labor camp, Kalman was liberated from the darkroom into the studio. Laci Kovacs, Varkonyi's assistant, took over the picture taking while Kalman talked to the clients. "He was fast and a good decision maker," says Kalman, "but he lacked the high school polish in his vocabulary and in his conversations." A leftist member of the proletariat, Kovacs teased Kalman, the bourgeois son of a newspaper editor. "But I learned quickly, we meshed and had good success." ■ When Kovacs was drafted (he died marching to Russia), Kalman was put in charge. Working every day until midnight, his eyes began popping out from what seemed to be Graves disease. That condition plus a dangerously high metabolism (thanks to gorging on sausage the day before the test) gave him a one-year

First Leica, 1941

reprieve from labor camp. A year later he repeated the dodge. He had better things to do and his family already had enough to worry about: brother Pista had been drafted into a labor camp and was working on the railroad in the Ukraine. ■ Despite the ever worsening political situation, Kalman enjoyed the company of actresses, artists and other independent-minded, "slightly cuckoo" theatre people. "No Jew dared get married at the time," he says, "but I could fall in and out of love." Love affairs in Hungary were not such a brouhaha as in moralistic America. ■ While on a ski trip to the Matra Mountains, Kalman

Béla poses here with other photography students who took their apprentice exams in the summer of 1940. He's the confident man holding the Leica in the center of the back row.

photographed two actresses wearing the latest ski apparel. Zoltan Egyed, the editor of the largest theatrical magazine in Hungary, published the photos in his fashion section the next week and told him, "Young man your place is in America." That would come much later. ■ On January 20, 1944 Kalman was called up for labor camp duty. Along with 400 other JANS, (an abbreviation for *Jelenleg Alkalmatlan*, which means "disabled at present"), his activities included unloading, sorting and tying fur vests returned from the Russian front and later packing and mailing army officers' uniforms. Still able to tune in to Radio Free Europe, Kalman and his mates smiled as they shipped parcels to towns already in the hands of the advancing Russians. ■ Although Kalman heard horror stories about friends and fellow labor campers disappearing and perishing in the gas chambers, the only blood he shed was from tightening strings when packing parcels. The fact that long hours and poor working conditions caused his eyeballs to protrude more and more concerned none of his superiors. "The aim of the labor camp was to do away with us. There was no mercy, indulgence or humanitarian behavior. Some sadists even accelerated our destruction by tortures. At that time even the words 'human dignity' could be found only in dictionaries." ■ Kalman was discharged in May of 1944, only to find that he would have to rejoin within a few weeks. To improve his chances of survival, he moved to his cousin Lili's home. The new address meant he would be assigned to a labor camp where the uncle of his apprentice, Karcsi Gink, was in charge. ■ Consequently, Kalman was not one of the more than 10,000 labor campers dispatched to Bor, Yugoslavia, and other places to clear war rubble and work the mines. Few ever returned. A half dozen times, Ensign Gink winked at Kalman and took him out of a marching company. "Otherwise there would be nobody in Budapest to help his nephew at the photographer apprentice's examination." ■ Gink spoke to Kalman only once, calling him a "silly ass" for making the near fatal mistake of going into town and getting a shave and haircut. Caught by gendarmes, he and a friend narrowly avoided the fate of other Jews in Jaszbereny and Szolnok, a trip to Auschwitz. Instead, they were sentenced to a week's labor shoveling out latrines. ■ On the Sunday following the landing at Normandy, Kalman and other campers marched out to the drill grounds where they saw Colonel "Ivan the Terrible" Zentay sitting on a horse ranting about "the stinking pig Jews" and "the new European order that would soon be born where gypsies, homosexuals, Slavs, mental patients and Jews would not exist to taint the air." ■ During the speech, Kalman saw the "heavenly spectacle" of vapor trails from American bombers destroying the Tisza bridge of Szolnok. "Seeing this and hearing the noise of the bombers, the horses began rearing. Labor campers fled in all directions but the intelligent horses didn't know that they could trample the Jews, unpunished. They avoided us gracefully and only pranced around." Kalman and colleagues then marched back to camp, laughing and humming "It's a long way to Tipperary." ■ Although the war was winding down, Nazi extermination efforts intensified, leaving Jews in greater danger than before. On August 20, Saint Steven's Day, Kalman traveled from Mizsepuszta to Pest by train and heard the agonized cries of Italian Jews crammed in a cattle car as they called for water, the horrible finale to the events he later saw dramatized in Vittorio De Sica's 1971 film *The Garden of the Finzi-Continis*. ■ Back at the camp, he and his brother, Pista, shoveled rubble and coal. Thanks to what Kalman calls "photography related bribery," the two were together at a camp close to their parents in Pest, a fact that made other families grumble about the "splendid deal rigged by the two smart brothers." ■ The two took chances. After completing a day's work, they changed out of their laborer's uniforms into air raid warden uniforms and headed home. Jews couldn't be air raid wardens; therefore, they were dressed as gentiles and could travel freely. ■ The Horthy Proclamation of October 15, 1944 led most Jews to believe that Germans would withdraw their troops from Hungary and Horthy would sign an armistice agreement with the Russians. Instead, the SS took Horthy prisoner for the crime of selling the country to the Bolsheviks and imperialists. The Kalman brothers quickly guessed "that the situation was not kosher" and went underground for several days before returning to labor camp. ■ On November 1, they heard gossip that the company would soon march for Germany. Taking the news seriously, they phoned a friend who picked up their rucksacks, then got up early the next morning. Wearing their air-raid warden uniforms, they dashed to a nearby bombed-out house and hid on the third floor, which they reached by hanging onto the intact side of a collapsed flight of stairs. There they heard the SS gendarmes barking; "Quicker, move quicker" as they hit men with their gunstocks. None of the men who marched off to Germany were seen again. ■ Béla and Pista completed their escape by

In 1941 Béla switched from Leica to a Contax Two camera.

impersonating rubble-clearing engineers. Holding measuring tape, notepads, red and blue pens and rolls of paper, they looked so official that policemen saluted them. At 8:30 that morning, they arrived home at their parents' place at Ujpesti-Quay, "thus ending our labor camp tour of duty in this Kingdom of Hungary." ■ Two days later, they donned their air-raid warden uniforms again and headed to the train station to "liberate" some food. Dodging bodies and bullets, Béla and Pista each brought home a big box of *Durrgemuese*, dehydrated carrot and turnip greens. The family would eat so much of this that neither brother ate carrots or turnips for the next ten years. ■ Kalman next became obsessed with obtaining a *Schutzpass* (safe conduct pass). First he looked to the Swiss Embassy, then to the Pope in Rome, only to find that the passes issued under their names were fake, printed by the Hungarian Resistance. When he heard that legitimate Spanish, Swedish and Portuguese protective passports could be obtained, his ears perked up. ■ Three years earlier, Kalman had photographed a christening ceremony for Angel Sans-Briz, then the third secretary of the Spanish Embassy. Sans-Briz was so pleased with the pictures that he hired Kalman to teach him to take snapshots of his baby daughter. ■ Word had it that the Franco government would give protective passports to Jews of Spanish origin who would repatriate to Spain at the end of war. As Kalman points out, such Jews were all over Europe. "In 1492 when this brave Christopher Columbus sailed toward east/west, tens of thousands of destitute Spanish Jews embarked too, but towards the Netherlands. From there, many went to Germany, Poland and Hungary. My Aunt Ilonka exemplified this Spanish strain." ■ The next day, Kalman headed to the consulate dressed as a Nazi Hungarian. To achieve the look he wore his father's World War I boots, leather gloves, hunter's breeches and jacket, and a Tyrolean hat decorated with wild hog bristles and a SS death's head badge. He carried a Nazi newspaper and an Austrian walking stick. ■ At the consulate, he insisted with all the arrogance a 23-year old could muster that he wished to speak personally to Mr. Sans-Briz, who was by then the ambassador. "It was not for nothing that I moved about so much among good actors," he says. Soon after, Kalman held four protective letters written in German, Hungarian and Spanish and a voucher to move into a protective apartment, at the international ghetto. ■ A few days later, he and Pista obtained false identification papers, including a certificate of baptism, from a former classmate. Thereafter, they kept Jewish papers in their left jacket pockets and the fake Christian papers in their right. Even so, Kalman found himself spat on and thrown off a street car for being Jewish. Worse, he and Pista barely escaped being shackled, shot and thrown into the Danube by Nazis who asked to see their identification papers after Pista was caught picking up an airdropped leaflet of Russian propaganda. ■ After this narrow escape, the Kalmans stayed in their protected house, playing poker, drinking watery tea, dining on *Durrgemuese*, and waiting for the closing of the Russian pincer attack around Pest and Buda. "When the day of liberation came both of us were at our slimmest in our lives." ■ On January 18, 1945, the day of liberation, Béla an Pista went down to Rudolf Square to celebrate the death of the fascist beast only to find that "these liberators of ours became impertinent, searching in pockets, coats and cap linings to liberate anything of value." Worse, men were herded off for Russian work details, some to return after three to five years, others not at all, and women were raped. ■ A few days later, Béla and Pista went to the party house at Tisza Kalman-Square to seek work, Pista (who spoke Russian), as an interpreter and Béla, as a photographer. ■ After proving his mettle with passport and building photographs, Béla began taking photos for the Russian Artillery Documentation Department. Wearing the cap and coat of a Russian officer, he traveled in open military trucks, ate goulash with the Russians, and recorded visible hits on the walls of the bombarded city. The 5,000 photographs he took were classified military secrets. On February 13, after the German surrender of Buda, Kalman saw 10,000 German corpses laid out at the Royal Castle courtyard but was not permitted to photograph them. ■ Once the Russians moved on to Berlin, Kalman was fired for trumped up reasons concocted by "a scoundrel who came up in the communist world quite well." Ever the survivor, he began taking publicity and press release photos of the new leadership. Comrade Vas was the new high commissioner in charge of the city's food supply and his office was in the new City Hall. Peter Kellemen, Vas's secretary, heard through the grapevine that Kalman was a nephew of his boss. Because paternalism was a strong ingredient of the new political scene, he arranged for Kalman to have two rooms in the basement of City Hall to do his photography. "I, of course, heard this rumor only behind my back and so I had no opportunity to refute it." ■ Kalman specialized in anything that was needed: mostly shots of parades, orators, factories, portraits. When the International Red Cross required a record of the victims of starvation and cold lying out on the sidewalks of the former ghetto, Kalman photographed the bodies with their name tags wired to their feet and yellow stars of David sewn on their clothes. He also ' documented the hanging of Rotyis and Szivos (sadistic service men who had murdered more than a thousand labor campers). ■ In May 1945, Kalman Foto was opened at Anker-koz No. 1, a prime downtown location. His new space was as big as the Varkonyi Studio and even more up to date. (Although Varkonyi had asked him to return, Kalman declined because he was not offered a 50 percent partnership). ■ Kalman Foto soon prospered thanks to theater and ballet world connections from the "old and bad capitalist days" of 1942. "We became a swinging, fashionable studio," says Béla, who photographed famous actors and actresses, displayed the photographs in the lobbies of theaters and published them in magazines. Every photo had a large Kalman "K" sticker on the bottom left. "The direction of the K directed your eyes to the image." Within a year, he was the official photographer for twelve theaters. ■ He soon photographed politicians as well, thanks to brother Pista, who had introduced him to Ivan Boldizsar, Press Secretary for the Coali-

Kalman Foto existed from 1945 to 1951 and was located on the sixth floor of the Anker Palace, a prime location in downtown Budapest.

The kinetic Kalman "K"—reproduced here from a page of letterhead—appeared on all photographs from the studio.

In 1947 Béla posed with his first flash—a Wabash Sylvania product. Its two wet cell batteries were good for 50 shots before recharging.

This triple portrait of Tolnay, Darvas and Varkonyi appeared on the cover of Film, Szinhaz Irodalom *magazine in 1947. When he fled to America in 1956, Kalman left behind most of his negatives and almost all of the theater and dance magazines in which he had published.*

tion Government. Bo, whom Kalman describes as a "slender, intense, dark-haired Adonis," sent him VIPs and other "smaller or greater demi-Gods from the political zoo of that time." Previously, the party leaders had been photographed by Funk Pal Angelo, a glamour photographer who indulged in heavy retouching. Kalman preferred to flatter his customers with good lighting and composition. ■ In 1948, he took up a new genre: graduation portraits known as tableau photographs. "We made a lot of money," he says. "I had 25 to 30 people working at the studio. And all of this, when I was 27 years young. What energy I had." Often clients didn't believe that such a young man was *the* Kalman, *the* photographer. Many asked, 'Where is your father, the famous Kalman?' " ■ By the end of the forties, Kalman Foto fell victim to politics and to the socialist planned economy. Theater work went to state-run photo studios and tableaus to state-owned cooperatives. As a member of the private sector, Kalman could employ only three to five workers and could procure only a limited amount of film and paper. ■ Kalman Foto closed in December 1951. "It was one of the bitterest pills of my life to swallow. The honeymoon lasted five years, the sixth was spent in fear that all I had accumulated would melt away. All my equipment, my negatives, my cameras went into the stock of the Feny-Szov (the state cooperative) and I never ever got a cent for them." ■ Kalman's 1951 income of approximately $500 a month shrank to a paycheck of $50, the highest possible for the category of "Outstanding Artistic Photographer." Seven days a week, he worked around the clock trying to achieve "the silly, pre-planned, impossible production quotas." He saw little of his family during the period, including his gravely ill father, who died in 1952 at age 68. ■ The work was routine and boring. "There was no need to think, only to be silent, nod our heads and accept their socialist ideas like manna from heaven. Composition, style, elan—what we today call zip— were denounced as capitalist remnants. They met intense resistance from our superiors." ■ In addition to producing propagandistic photo-graphs, Kalman had to recite Majakovszki's adulatory poem *Lenin* and play the part of an exploitative, slave-owning Texas farmer in a propaganda play. "All this was so I would not be seen in conflict with a system that I hated from the bottom of my heart. We knew about the Gulag but we didn't speak about it." ■ Kalman believes he survived because of his sense of humor and headstrong nature. "I could from time to time smile or laugh and sometimes made quips in rhyme." Given his capitalist, bourgeois background, he was lucky to have kept the three-room apartment he shared with his mother and not be transported to Recsk, the Hungarian Gulag, for former capitalists. ■ To make more money and stay active, Kalman invented extracurricular projects that had to be approved by the censors, the State Fine Art Foundations' Jury. One project was a series of photographs entitled *Immortal Lovers*. Actors, actresses, singers and dancers from the theater, opera and ballet appeared before his lens, posed in period costumes as Anthony and Cleopatra, Romeo and Juliet and other great lovers. The 15,000 forints he earned

Kalman Foto's advertisements were striking examples
of Bauhaus graphics. In contrast, the reception area
featured luxurious Louis XIV furniture.
In the studio scene at bottom left, Béla adjusts the head
of a model as part of a portrait session.

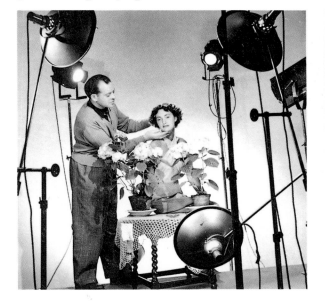

FOTO KÁLMÁN

DEÁK-TÉR, ANKER PALOTA   22-66-87.

These 1952 snaps show Béla and his coworkers in the state photo cooperative known as Feny Szov.

Although the socialist regime forced the closing of Kalman Foto, Béla continued to produce prize-winning products. In the photograph above, he celebrates winning the "Best Studio Award" with other members of the State Enterprise Winning Team. Below, Béla marches in the May Day Parade. Official patriotic activities were part of the job description.

for his first series of six pictures represented half a year's salary at the photo factory where he slaved by day. During the next two years, he completed twenty series, earning 120,000 forints. "Taking these pictures was a real joy because I had been kept from theatrical photography for five years. The actors, these talented immoral bums, were people close to my heart." ■ In 1955, Kalman's personal projects were put on hold while he trained to be an army photosurveillance specialist at a campsite southwest of the Danube. At the end of three months, he was promoted to the rank of master sergeant of the Hungarian Peoples Army. ■ Kalman's final project completed in Hungary was a book of ballet photographs begun in 1954. Although published in 1956, it was shredded shortly after. The reason was simple: the dancers left in November 1956 and so did the photographer. An embarrassment to the state. ■ On the evening of October 23, 1956, Béla and a friend left the beer hall of the Beke Hotel, when an army tank sped by with soldiers on top waving the Hungarian tricolor flag and wondered "what the hell was going on." ■ Kalman had seen the student demonstrations on Bem Apó Square in Buda that afternoon but had not made too much of it. Unknown to him, the demonstrators had moved on, first to take over the Sandor Street State Radio Station and then to the park where they toppled the giant 40 foot statue of Stalin. ■ The next day, Kalman saw "our good father Stalin's nose in the dirt on the front pages of our newspapers" and heard reports of a revolution. Looking out from the top floor of his building, he saw nothing: no cars, no tanks, no people on the streets. ■ Three days later, he and an unexpected visitor found themselves in the line of fire. A freedom fighter had thrown a Molotov cocktail from the top floor of their building, destroyed a Russian weapons' carrier and incinerated the driver. Three tanks responded by spraying the top floor of their building with machine gun fire. The two escaped by lying flat on the floor of the kitchen, away from the street. "It was extremely frightening," Kalman remembers. "In a split second we turned all white from the plaster dust falling from the ceiling." ■ A few days later Kalman installed new windows thanks to his "good connections," waited for his mother to return from the hospital where she had been undergoing tests and treatments, and began seriously contemplating joining the ranks of those fleeing to Austria. ■ First, he would take some unforgettable pictures. On October 30, Béla's assistant phoned him with the news that he stole an automobile and Russian papers and was about to go to the Parliament. Once they started photographing there, word came that two army majors had freed Cardinal Jozsef Mindszenty, who had been under house arrest since 1949. Kalman took photos of the cardinal and also photographed Imre Nagy, Pal Maleter, Zoltan Tildy, Ferenc Erdei, Geza Losonczy, Anna Kethly and others. "Never did I imagine at that point that *Life* magazine would buy the entire material in a few weeks time." ■ Kalman rejoiced at Hungary's new-found freedom, then witnessed the brutal return of the Russians. "Khrushchev sent 6,000 tanks for our protection against the revolution which was renamed 'counterrevolution,' a good excuse to crush it." ■ In despair, he listened to the rumors about taxis and trucks taking people over the border for reasonable fees of 5,000-10,000 Forints. Although he heard stories about those who were caught and labeled "enemy of the people," the Russians seemed to have little interest in stopping the mass exodus. ■ Once he decided to leave, Kalman acted quickly. He and a traveling companion bought train tickets to Sopron and dressed casually as if making a trip to the country. An official-looking letter from Feny-Szov authorized him to take photographs at an International Exhibit in Sopron. "This was a fake note. I typed it. I wrote it. I signed our two bosses' names on the bottom and put a big State Enterprise Company stamp on it." Hidden in his jacket were the negatives he had taken at the parliament—"a real danger in case I was caught." ■ Pulling out of the station on November 20, Kalman had no regrets. "I was 35 years old looking ahead toward a new life with great expectations. The future could only be better. I felt no regret at leaving my repeatedly cheated and fooled, poor, old country." ■ He and his companion rode in second class on the train, sitting on wooden seats "as there was no first class anything in this people's democracy." At Komarom, everyone got off the train and spent the night in a waiting room. At Gyor, he booked a room in a hotel, had breakfast, took in some scenery and arranged for a taxi for the trip to the Austrian border. ■ When the taxi failed to arrive, they started walking. "All of a sudden, a canvas covered Russian truck came to a screeching halt next to us. Two machine gunners jumped out and wondered if we wanted to sleep in Vienna the next night?" Frightened, Kalman replied that he and his companion were going to Sopron to do jury duty. " 'Trust us,' the Russian said. 'Look here' and he pulled up the cover of the truck. There they sat, a dozen future escapees crammed on wooden benches. 'Come on up and let's go. 5,000 forints.' " ■ Kalman and his companion declined the offer and walked until picked up by a hay truck charging 10,000 forints to the border. "We thought, for so much money, this is going to be true and okay." ■ "What did we know about where the border was?" The peasant dropped them off in the middle of a field that turned out to be a mile from the border zone but fourteen miles to the border. Walking in the snow, sleeping under bridges, ducking shots from machine gunners, listening to crying and screams, Kalman dragged himself across rough terrain despite a swollen, badly sprained ankle. Finally, he crossed the 45 foot canal into Austria on a jerryrigged bridge of wood planks and posts. The once insignificant little bridge at Andau—made famous by Michener's bestselling account—had been destroyed by the Russians only a few days before. ■ "Welcome, you are free," said the Austrian guards in Hungarian at the border. Taking two Kossuth silver coins out of his pocket, Kalman gave one to each of the guards. "They stared at these, never having received anything but handshakes or hugs." ■ Limping towards the village of Andau, Kalman and his companion met a couple with a two seater Fiat who came from Vienna every night to help. After a treat of coffee and chocolate, they squeezed into

Colonel Pal Maleter's defection to the freedom fighters' cause elevated him to the status of national hero. He inspired his men to face the Soviet tanks with great courage and asked his men to call him "Friend" not "Sir." The six foot six inch hero was executed on Khrushchev's orders on June 16, 1958. When Béla sent a copy of this 1956 photograph to Maleter's widow, she thanked him and said it was the last photograph ever taken of him.

When Kalman fled Hungary, he risked his life by taking these photographs of Cardinal Mindszenty and other "enemies of the state" in his pocket. The works were bought by Life *magazine and exhibited in the lobby of Rockefeller Center in 1958.*

On October 30, 1956—one week before the Russians returned to brutally end the Hungarian Revolution—Kalman photographed the members of Prime Minister Imre Nagy's short-lived government. This photograph of Nagy, who was executed in 1958, was made into a stamp in Greece that year.

Shortly after he arrived in American in late December 1956, Kalman joined a demonstration at the United Nations protesting the brutal Russian invasion of Hungary. There he photographed actor Charles Corvin reciting the Petofi poem "Hungarians rise/Here's the time now or never."

the luggage compartment for the drive to Vienna. Holed up in the flat of his second cousin with 18 other refugees, he nursed his swollen ankle and thought ruefully about not taking one of the Russian trucks with the "squeaky tires and even squeakier offers." They had delivered their passengers safely days before. ■ Kalman called home the next morning to announce he had arrived safely and called his Aunt Ilonka in Chicago to see if she would sponsor his trip to America. She would. Ten long days of queues and bureaucratic paperwork followed with the Viennese police and the United States consulate. "Speaking in English, I had to tell story after story of my life. They went back to the same question a dozen times asking it in different ways: Which party was I a member of? The Americans were paranoid because of rumors circulating about Hungarian Communists trying to get to the U.S. to perform sabotage activities."
■ Kalman confessed to briefly—and unwillingly—joining the National Peasants Party in 1947. That year a representative advised him to join the party if he wished to continue work as the party photographer. "This was the extent of my party activity between 1945 and 1956," he says. "I also told them about how they called me a decadent, antisocial, formalist, America-imitator and a Hollywood-styled capitalist star photographer who related very poorly to the people's democratic system." ■ To obtain transportation to the United States, Kalman headed to the Hebrew Immigrant Aid Society (HIAS), where approximately 15,000 Jews were lined up—"everyone I knew from Pest." When word came that nobody was on line at the Protestant organization offices, Kalman thought, "Why couldn't I be a Protestant? I had to pretend for twelve years that I was not Jewish." ■ Kalman walked over to the World Church Service Office, which sponsored Lutheran and Protestant refugees, and was on their list in five minutes. He received his American visa on December 10 and thanked Vice President Nixon, who had been sent to Vienna by Eisenhower to study the Hungarian refugee situation shortly after Anna Kethly, Hungary's U.N. Representative, spoke out against the Russian aggression at the United Nations. ■ After taking a bus to Frankfurt, Kalman flew to Shannon, Ireland, then on to Newfoundland and Camp Kilmer, New Jersey, where he and his fellow refugees were greeted by second and third generation Hungarian-American soldiers. ■ "I was the only one in my group of 40 people who understood these Hungarian Yankees," Kalman remembers. "Since I was able to speak English I replied to their many instructions and became the center of communication." Soon he was meeting old friends, such as Istvan Barankovics, a pre-communist era politician whose portrait he had taken in Budapest, and Pal Javor, a Hungarian actor. Barankovics was soon shouting, "Of course, I remember Kalman Foto. Kalman Foto is here. Boy, do we need you." Javor agreed: "How smart of you to come here. This country is the right place for your talent." ■ Thanks to Javor, Kalman learned that he had relatives in New York City and decided to celebrate the Christmas holidays there. "It was all talk of Hungary. Who is alive? Who is doing what and where? How was the revolution? How did

I escape." ■ Itching to photograph again, Kalman borrowed a Rollei and joined a demonstration at the United Nations protesting the Soviet invasion of Hungary. There he met Martin Munkacsi, the Hungarian-born photographer and *bon vivant* whom he had long considered "the Great White Hope." "By that time Martin had been fired from *Vogue* and did not take pictures anymore. He came to the demonstration as a good patriot." ■ Although his New York family gave him many gifts, for Béla the greatest Christmas gift was America. On December 26 he took a Greyhound bus for Chicago and moved in with his Aunt Ilonka and Uncle Rudi, who lived on the first floor of a home once used by the German Consulate. (A mosaic swastika was kept well covered with carpet.) ■ "They heard from the horse's mouth the entire story of the uprising and the times right afterwards when western journalists could not report the developments any more. But that was the past and I was looking forward to the future. I had been quite idle for almost three months and was eager to work again." ■ He began work thanks to his cousin Georgette, who had been his first employee in Budapest in May 1945. She had already called various Chicago studios looking for leads and had set up interviews at studios interested in "a Hungarian freedom fighter photographer, master and medal winner." ■ Kalman's American career began in the "empire" of Wesley Bowman, a commercial photographer whose clients in the late '50s included the Leo Burnett Company, Spiegels, and Carson, Pirie and Scott. "Bowman was fascinated with my story and I was fascinated with his empire and with the fact that he did not even know which end of the camera had the lens." Bowman hired him at $2.00 an hour. "All over the country my fellow refugee Hungarian photographers got jobs for $1.50 per hour." ■ Washing and drying 8×10 inch prints, 400 per hour, eight hours per day was a "Sisyphean ordeal," not that different from sorting fur vests at the labor camp in Hungary. Looking on the light side, Béla compared himself to Charlie Chaplin in *Modern Times*. ■ To stave off boredom, he noted the way other employees tackled fashion and other assignments and spent his weekends photographing, making personal images and photographing weddings. After several weeks, he began assisting Erik Sorensen, a Danish-born cameraman who had arrived in America eight years before, and worked mostly on the Marlboro cigarette account. ■ Although Kalman's fame in Hungary had rested on his portraits, he decided that in America the future lay in commercial photography. "There was only one big portrait studio and that was the Bachrach Studio. Their posings were so artificial, their work so heavily retouched that I thought if this is the highest in portraiture in America then that's a step back for me." ■ After three or four months learning the ropes at the Bowman empire, Kalman took another job, quit it after only a few weeks, then spent a year working as a photographic illustrator for Nugent/Williams, a Chicago mail order house. Its 60,000 square foot space offered 12 studios for 24 photographers. In addition, commercial artists did layouts and air-brushed the indecencies out of corsets and petticoats. ■ Kalman's

On assignment for Life, *Chicago, 1957.*

coworkers claimed they loved photography but few interrupted the fun of fishing, flying kites and playing with their kids and dogs to snap pictures on Saturdays and Sundays. "I was sort of weird for them," Kalman says. "I came back from doing photography on my own and developed my pictures on Mondays after hours." ■ That year Kalman bought his first car, a used 1955 Chevy Bel Air. He also met and dated a Japanese voice student named Yukiko Murata from Hiroshima. Although his aunt tried to introduce him to Jewish women, he preferred being with Yuki, and learning about a "whole new culture, habits, foods, manners and new perspective of a world without Jews." They took frequent trips around Illinois and Indiana and married a year later. ■ "Love, car, job, health. What else was there?" Having kept in touch with other Hungarian photographers from the state enterprise, he compared notes and concluded that at $165 a week he was "among the highest paid and in the most pleasant of jobs." ■ That said, Kalman decided that he would prefer a stint with *Life* magazine over more time at the catalogue house on Pulaski Road. Kalman wrote to Henry Luce at Time/Life to ask for a job and was told to report to *Life*'s Chicago bureau. Full-time jobs were not available but free-lance assignments were possible. "I put on my thinking cap and within a week I presented six different story ideas." They accepted one, "Hungarians A Year After," meaning a year after settling in the United States. Who were they? What did they do? That fall, Kalman took time off and went on the road with a reporter. ■ "It was the hardest six weeks of my entire working life," he says. "We had to visit twenty people all over the states to photograph them and to interview them. Our schedule was deadly but all *Life* people live and work like that and they love it." ■ The marathon effort brought him "a 16 pound weight loss, $1,600 dollars in the bank, 16,000 photos and 16 finalists selected to illustrate the story." Scheduled to run on the first anniversary of the Hungarian Revolution, it was preempted by a story on the fortieth anniversary of the Russian Revolution. ■ Kalman—who had wanted to work for *Life* ever since his family picked photography as his career—was disappointed but learned an important lesson: "I never, ever wanted to work for *Life* again. It's criminally insane the way they work. Shoot, shoot, shoot. One good picture out of a thousand. Not a good ratio. No artistry to it. It is deadly, hard and frustrating and at best a story had a life of only one week." ■ Back at Nugent/Williams, Kalman faced the challenge of photographing Easter bunnies facing left to right for the new catalog, the reverse of the previous year's approach. "The little Easter rabbit did it. I calmly walked into the studio manager's office and served notice! I was free again and not a slave of another commerical warlord. It was sweet and I felt good about being able to quit when and if I felt so." ■ Soon after, Béla and Yuki took off in the gray Chevy to attend the opening of a *Life* magazine exhibition of photos by Hungarian photographers (Béla included) displayed in the lobby of Rockefeller Center. There Henry Luce advised him to try again. "He said I might just get a cover story.

How nice it would have been, but I was not interested any more in working for *Life*." In fact, he tried one more time, photographing dancer Margot Fonteyn. It was not printed either. ■ At the exhibition in New York, Kalman met Robert Halmi, a Hungarian emigre photographer who had gone to Hollywood in the 1940s. With four other men, they formed the Halmi Group of Photographers based at 45 West 56th Street. "It was an unfortunate venture," he says. "Too many chiefs and no Indians but me. No one else spoke much English so I took every phone call. I was interrupted so often that I worked late into the night."
■ Although they photographed Katherine Hepburn and other stars, work was generally tedious. He slaved 100 hours a week and made a meager $100. "For this I did not have to come to the Big Apple. I was sorry about the move and forming a company with Hungarians who were okay in Budapest but totally lost in New York City. I'd gone from the tepid Communist way of working to working myself to smithereens in New York. I did not want to die of a heart attack at age 37." ■ After quitting the Halmi Group, Kalman learned "a few good lessons about life in a capitalist society." One such venture was "Mr. Béla's Magic Lens."
■ "I fell into the trap of photographing in the Catskill Mountains at a hotel called Evans," he says. With partners Laci and Susan Almasi he bought the rights to photograph hotel guests for $1,000 with the promise that they would make $10,000 by summer's end. The plan was to photograph 200 guests at the pool, dinner, tennis, etc., then sell them souvenir pictures. The three worked around the clock, Béla photographing people until midnight, Laci developing the rolls overnight, and Susan taking orders the next day. ■ Back from the Catskills where Mr. Béla's magic lens had produced a little money for a lot of effort, he and Laci began photographing Madison Avenue shop windows at night. Working entirely "on spec," they offered prints at $2 per picture the next morning. Those not purchased were ripped up. By noon, they usually made $30 to $40 and enjoyed a free afternoon. ■ Tired of the hustle, Kalman joined the Lewis Studio in East Orange, New Jersey. The owner, Donald Hults, was a superb salesman who could talk for hours to future clients. Back in the studio, however, he turned into a "Prussian artillery colonel—fast, forward, impatient, demanding and intolerant." Eyeing the studio operation, Kalman missed little. When he opened his own business in Boston a few years later, he copied the entire setup from types of equipment to order forms, price lists and publicity. ■ Near the end of 1959, Kalman read an ad in the *New York Times*: "New England's largest photo studio looking for a creative advertising photographer with years of studio experience. Ask for Harry." He called, sent his resume and traveled to Boston for an interview. "I was unique with my migratory directions," says Kalman, "and the people at Fay Photo looked curiously at this Hungarian who wanted to come from New York City to Boston."
■ On March 15, 1960 he reported to Fay Photo for work. "Was I glad to leave Kaiser Wilhelm Hults and his Prussian staff for this charming old world town." Yuki decided not to follow Béla to Boston and they

Kalman bought Studio 350, located at 350 Newbury Street in downtown Boston, in 1966.

Béla met his future wife Edna when she bought this solarized flower picture in 1964.

All in a day's work. On location, 1956.

divorced a year later. ▪ Fay Photo had recently bought 350 Newbury Street and renovated the building into studios, darkrooms, kitchen, and conference rooms. Kalman's starting salary was $200 a week with no overtime pay. "Right away, everyone wanted their work done only by me, so the good start soured soon." One member left to form his own studio though Béla thought his work needed "creative juice." His own creativity meanwhile attracted clients, many of whom would stick with him for 25 years. ▪ In 1962, Kalman became a U.S. citizen, applied for a passport, and traveled back to the old country. In Baden bei Wien, Austria, he met his brother, Pista, and his mother (then 78 and ill with Parkinson's Disease), who had been granted permission to undergo treatments at the spa. As the rich uncle from America, Béla paid for everything. After his mother returned to Budapest, where she died a year later, the brothers traveled to Italy. ▪ In April 1964 Kalman exhibited 15 color prints at the Weeden Gallery in Boston, and sold a solarized flower photo to an enthusiastic, radiant collector named Edna, whom he had met at the opening of another show. A year later, on December 17, 1965 Béla and Edna were married at Temple Ohabei Shalom. With Edna's children, Abby, 10, and Eric, 8, they departed for St. Croix for a honeymoon of snorkeling and sailing. Being a family man was a new experience for Béla and "a dear one." The workaholic made sure he was home every night for dinner by 6:30. ▪ The next summer, Kalman bought Studio 350 from Fay Photo. Although it took years to distance himself away from the handshake, banquet and publicity picture-taking reputation of Fay Photo, Kalman gained a reputation for creative portraiture and advertising. ▪ The studio was booked for weeks ahead and he worked fast and furiously every day. Constructing sets, arranging props, preparing food, arranging flowers, going out on location—there was never a dull moment. Photographing Baskin and Robbins frappes and fantasies, they kept ten gallon containers of all 31 flavors. Working for Keyes-Fiber, they acquired a ten year supply of paper cups and plates. And once they had to select "the right and perfect donut from over 2,000 for Dunkin Donuts." Honeywell, Hood Milk, Stop & Shop, Sheraton, Frye Boots, Stride Rite, Houghton Mifflin, Rust Craft, Polaroid, Boston Ballet and United Fruit were a few of the clients. Over

the years, Kalman won many Art Director Club awards. ■ "I satisfied lots of art directors and their whims. It all required amazing amounts of energy. I deserved my dinner every night." Béla delegated jobs yet knew how to do all parts of the operation himself. "It was always team-work at the studio but I had the privilege to push the button." he says. "I tried to be the best boss because I'd been an employee for so many years." ■ Despite the success, accounts came and went. "You are only good for that shining 15 seconds, not as Andy Warhol has said, 15 minutes," says Kalman. "The art director handling a million dollar account could be the most powerful man one day and be fired the next." During his last few years at Studio 350, he lost five major accounts. At age 62, it was time to move on, to grow in creative, noncommerical new ways. ■ Now 72, Béla Kalman prides himself on his ability to look at the world with an open, young and agile mind. "It's important for a photographer not to get stuck in a box. Creativity will be my slogan forever. Retire, never!" ■ Back in 1956, Kalman's first book on Hungarian ballet dancers fell victim to the revolution. His second book *Angkor: Monuments of the God Kings* (1975), fared better. In the late six-ties, Kalman read in the newspaper that Jacqueline Kennedy Onassis had traveled to the Far East and was frustrated because she could not buy a high quality color book depicting the ruins at Angkor Wat. ■ Kalman decided to provide it. Because professional photographers were not per-mitted to work at the ruins, he applied for a visitor's visa. Traveling with Edna, he played the tourist carrying two Hasselblads, several lenses and fifty rolls of film. After four days traveling with an English-speaking guide and riding in a three-wheeled pedicab around the ruins, he made 1,200 negatives. Back in the states, it took one day to sell the project to the publishing firm of Harry N. Abrams. ■ For his next book, *Indian Country* (1987), Kalman toured the four corner area of New Mexico, Arizona, Utah and Colorado by foot, car and airplane, and made a total of 15,000 images. The project proved surprisingly hard to sell. Forty pub-lishers turned it down before Northland Press took it on. It is now in its third edition. ■ In 1985, Kalman noted that 1987 would be the twen-tieth anniversary of the Six Day War and decided to do a book com-memorating the unification of the Holy City of Jerusalem. He spent two months at a city guest house known as Mishkenot Shaananim (Peaceful Resting Place) but says, "There was no rest for me!" With an Israeli interpreter and driver, he "covered every nook and cranny of the Holy City" and made 3,000 images. ■ So far, the book has not been pub-lished. "A small historical glitch called Intifada got into the agenda on December 7, 1987 and it is still going on. Arabs, Christians and Jews are not living peacefully side by side, thus making the premise fiction."
■ Kalman's next book will be *Travels in Tuscany*. Although the project officially dates from 1988, Kalman traces his love of Italy and the Renais-sance back to this childhood when his father brought home nearly every art book published in Hungary. As a teenager, Béla studied Italian in school, Renaissance art at home and read *Vasari's Diary* in the original.

The crew of Studio 350. From left, Gabor, Béla, Jeff, Glenn.

A food photography assignment, 1977.

With Gyuri Kepes, 1982.

Béla with Eliot Porter in his studio in Tesuque, 1979.

Andrea Mantegna and Donato Bramante were favorite painters and a term paper involved comparing equestrian sculptures by Donatello and Andrea del Verrocchio. Best of all, in 1935, he attended summer school at the International School in Perugia. "So in 1988, when I was focusing on what to do next, it was easy to decide to revisit these cherished art pieces and plan an assignment photographing Tuscany's treasures." ▩ On working trips, Kalman is focused and driven. Knowing he won't be back right away, he pushes himself to accomplish as much as possible. "Once he has achieved that goal, he rests content," says Edna Kalman. "When he gets something good, he says 'That's a winner.'" ▩ Off duty at home or abroad, Kalman carries a camera, ever reminding himself, "Don't leave home without it." When he spots something to photograph he acts quickly. "See it. Take it. Love at first sight. When I see something with my three eyes, I develop the theme then and there." ▩ Kalman has never wanted to photograph suffering. "I'm only interested in beauty," he says. "I saw so much that was horrible during the war years and afterwards. I'm not talking just about blood, corpses and innocent people becoming statistics but also about greed, deceit and other forms of ugliness. It might seem aristocratic of me to show only beautiful things, but I feel mankind turns away from gore. What's beautiful has a greater chance to enlighten people spiritually." ▩ An extrovert, Kalman meets people in every city he visits. He counts many artists as close friends, but none closer than Gyorgy Kepes, the painter, photographer and author of *Language of Vision* (1944). Kepes (born 1906) became involved with another great Hungarian, Laszlo Moholy-Nagy (1895-1946), in the 1920s in Berlin. He then accompanied Moholy to the United States and became a member of the founding faculty of the New Bauhaus in Chicago. ▩ Kalman first met Kepes at an opening at the Museum of Science in Boston in 1971. Kepes—then recently retired from his professorship at the Massachusetts Institute of Technology— needed a darkroom. Kalman was happy to help. "It was like the Pope coming to you and saying 'Can I make a mass?'" A couple of days later, Kepes came with a suitcase full of twigs, wires, springs, lucite rods, negatives and other objects and started making exposures. The two soon became friends, sharing Japanese and Thai lunches, speaking Hungarian, discussing the old country and stimulating each other's work. "To me, he's the revered master. I'm his pal, his Hungarian connection," Kalman says. ▩ Kepes has described himself as "a seer not a stater," a point of view espoused by Kalman as well. With Kepes around, Kalman saw the "probabilities and possibilities of photograms," a medium that is well suited to exploring principles of light, transparency and motion. ▩ "I can't say Gyuri *changed* his work," says Edna Kalman thoughtfully, "but there was excitement in the contact." Adds Béla, laughing at his own vivid powers of exaggeration: "What I *really* learned is that photograms are not premeditated murder. Do it as you go. Trial and error." ▩ Serendipity has long played a role in his work. Back in 1942, Béla saw his apprentice Karcsi Gink accidentally photograph an actress at the moment when a drop of sweat ran down her heavily made up cheek. Because the sweat looked like a teardrop, the photo became a memorable theater poster. "This accident began Karcsi's career," says Kalman. "Since then I've learned to catch the rare, never-returning moment." ■ An avid experimenter, Kalman creates photographs that vary greatly in look and theme. "Béla doesn't like to remain static," says Edna. "Some people find a formula. He would rather try different things and stretch himself." ■ Kalman has taken cues from other artists and has honored Georges de la Tour, Frida Kahlo, Georgia O'Keeffe, René Magritte, Eliot Porter and others with photographic homages. Though not a copy cat, he tries out the visions of different imagemakers with a frisky spirit. "Man Ray was great with photograms. Let's see what Béla can do with photograms. Irving Penn creates beautiful flowers. Let's see what Béla can do with flowers. I'm constantly watching the so-called competition. That's an important part of development: watching the kid in the next sandbox building castles." ■ Unlike many artists, Kalman cares little about being the first with the latest. On the contrary, if he sees something he likes by another artist, he'll try to top it. Similarly, he has no interest in staking claim to a specific subject. Andy Warhol may have patented the soup cans, Roy Lichtenstein the comic strip, and Hilla and Bernd Becher typologies of coal breakers, but Kalman considers the whole world grist for his imagination. "Things are here for everyone," he says. "What fascinates me about photography is that no two photographs are alike. There is never something to get bored with. That keeps me alert and makes my creative juices flow." ■ In 1962, long before color photography was accepted as an art form, Kalman built a color darkroom. "I've battled and battled with people who say, 'real artists' compose in black and white. Those old hats; why should I do black and white when the world is in living color?" ■ Kalman regularly visits museums, galleries and studios. He subscribes to dozens of art, photography and general interest magazines and keeps up with technical developments. "The more you know the merrier, the brighter your scope is." He fights censorship, is glad that "nothing is sacred anymore" and believes that "the big filter is time." ■ An avid reader, he devours biography, history and occasional fiction but not mysteries. "I have too much respect for human life to read about fantastic methods by which someone is strangled or shot," he says. The sole exceptions are the whodunits penned by his friend Tony Hillerman. Keen on collecting, Kalman has amassed 4,000 art and photography books, 200 unusual photographs, as well as paintings, sculptures, stamps, bolos and cowboy boots. ■ During the past few years, Kalman has taken an increasing interest in the up-and-coming careers of young photographers, offering advice and sometimes buying their work. "I think a lot of people regard Béla as the grand old man of photography," says Edna. "He's had a lot of time to reflect on images and their meaning. People listen to what he has to say and he's never shy about saying it." ■ Nor has Kalman been shy about promoting his work. "Living in America, I've become a

Yousuf Karsh, 1959. "I took pictures of him in his style—shiny skin, pensive pose, relaxed mood," says Kalman. "He liked it and thanked me in a nice and kind letter."

In Indian Country, 1985. (Photograph by Paul Logsdon)

179

Though he has never held a full-time teaching post, Béla has long loved to meet and talk with students and other emerging photographers. Of a popular seminar on portrait and advertising photography he taught one semester at the College of Santa Fe in 1986, photographer David Scheinbaum said simply, "He was Béla."

In 1983 Kalman enjoyed a major retrospective exhibition at the Castle in Buda and appeared on television.

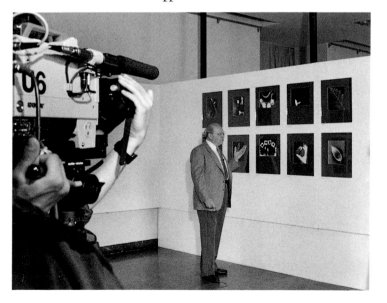

believer in that proverb 'If you don't toot your own horn, no one will toot it for you.'" Soon after arriving in Chicago in 1956, he showed his portfolio to Peter Pollack at the Art Institute of Chicago. Pollack's successor, Hugh Edwards, bought five of Kalman's Boston scenes at $5 each, telling him that Alfred Stieglitz had paid that sum for photographs by Eliot Porter and Edward Steichen. "I did not argue," says Kalman, "since it was the first museum in the new world to purchase my work for their collection. Now I have 24 museums on my list." ■ He has shown widely at art and photography galleries since the early sixties and in 1990 enjoyed a retrospective exhibition at the College of Santa Fe and University of Massachusetts Art Gallery in Boston. Most satisfying of all was his triumphant return to Hungary in 1983 to exhibit at the Castle Museum in Buda. ■ For years some Hungarian friends thought he betrayed the fatherland by leaving in 1956—along with 200,000 artists, photographers, writers, architects, lawyers, engineers, scientists and others—instead of staying for the struggle. No more. "Now that they are not afraid of censorship and can speak freely, I get letters saying, 'You were right to leave. What is called democracy here is worse than communism and as oppressive as before.' ■ "Had I stayed in that little country I would have been always saying 'I can't get film,' 'I can't travel abroad,' 'I can't do this and that' and always hitting my head against the wall. I felt I had to stay strong and fly and I did." ■ Kalman hopes his 55 plus years in photography will move the history of photography a notch or two ahead. "That will make it all worthwhile. I'm not a big fish, not a talent of unbelievable proportions, but that doesn't bother me because I feel I did very well for my size. In the great mosaic of photography, every one of us adds a little stone of color, shape and sparkle to the final design."

The National Gallery's Mobile Project discussion with
Alexander Calder and Paul Matisse in Cambridge, MA, 1976.

Meeting with Victor Hasselblad (R), Boston, 1978.

Béla and André Kertész in Santa Fe in 1984. Kertész
left Hungary in 1925, when Béla was only four years old.

A conversation with Beaumont Newhall
and Walter Chappell in 1990.

Wedding Bells, 1965. Abby,
Eric, Edna and Béla.

With Marie Cosindas at the Naylor
Camera Museum, Brookline, MA, 1982.

*Béla met Emperor Akihito
(then Crown Prince) in Tokyo in 1986.*

*Béla was a proud grandpa when he held his first grandson,
Alexander, in 1987. At left is his daughter in law Elizabeth.*

Béla with grandson Alexander, 1992.
Béla with his second grandson, Isaac, 1993.

SELECTED COLLECTIONS

Art Institute of Chicago

Brockton Art Museum, Brockton, MA.

Budapest Historic Museum

College of Santa Fe, Santa Fe, NM.

Federation of International Art
Photographers (FIAP)
Collection, Brussels

Hungarian Photo Artists Collection,
Budapest

Hungarian Photography Museum,
Kecskemet

Janus Pannonius Museum,
Pecs, Hungary

Museum of Fine Arts, Boston

Fine Arts Museum, Santa Fe, NM

National Gallery of Hungary, Budapest

Photographic Resource Center
at Boston University, Boston, MA

Polaroid Corporation, Cambridge, MA

Theater History Museum, Budapest

Tirgu Mures Photo Guild, Romania

Tornyai Janos Museum,
Hodmezovasarhely, Hungary

Worcester Art Museum,
Worcester, MA

Yildiz University Art Collection
Istanbul, Turkey

In southwestern attire, 1992.

BÉLA KALMAN, MFIAP

■ Kalman was given the title of Master in the Federation of International Artistic Photographers (MFIAP) in 1984. Now under the aegis of UNESCO, the Brussels-based group organizes photography exhibits that appear all over the world. The group reserves the title of Master for only 25 photographers at any given time and appointments are for life. Kalman's interest in FIAP dates back to the mid fifties when he was still living in Hungary. In 1955 he became an Associate of FIAP after having more than a hundred photographs accepted for exhibition during the past two years. In 1972 he began participating again, this time as an American, and advanced to the rank of Fellow. In 1984, a jury evaluated a group of 24 of his photographs (including many of his zoom lens photographs) and honored him with the title Master. Kalman is the only Master of FIAP from the United States. ■ Over the years Kalman has won 17 medals and exhibited his work in museums, galleries and art centers around the world. In 1983 at the invitational of the Ministry of Culture in Hungary, he has shown his work at three Hungarian museums. Since 1989 he has enjoyed major retrospective exhibitions at the University of Massachusetts Art Gallery in Boston, the College of Santa Fe Art Department Gallery and the Yildiz University Photography Gallery in Istanbul. Recent group exhibitions include *Southwest '90* and *In Camera: Photography and the Interior* at the Museum of Fine Arts In Santa Fe. In 1993 Kalman's photographs were displayed in the cities of Kecskemet and Eger in Hungary and Tirgu Mures in Romania.

ACKNOWLEDGMENTS

This book came about thanks to a great many people. ■ First and foremost, I am grateful to Edna, my wife of almost 30 years, for her love and support. She inspired many of the best photographs, read every caption and page of text and helped select the photographs. ■ My good friend Bill Field created and designed *The Third Eye*. He is the best designer I know, and I've had the pleasure of collaborating with him since the early 1960s when Boston's *Art Direction* magazine picked us as Artists of the Year and featured our images on facing pages. In 1990 Bill attended the opening of my retrospective exhibit *Fifty Years in Photography* at the College of Santa Fe, looked at the exhibition and said to Edna and me, "This is the history of photography through one man's lens. It should become a book." It took him three years to convince us to pursue the project but here it is: one man's history of photography from carbro to electronic in 55 years. "Sam" Field, Willy Field, Kate Field, Fred Cisneros, and Mindy Holmes assisted on this project with great competence and good cheer. ■ Many thanks to Van Deren Coke, Clifford Ackley, and Gyuri Kepes for their kind words and friendship. ■ Sally Eauclaire did a superb job writing the text and captions. Her text is not arty double talk, her English is impeccable, and she caught the essence of my message in her colorful essays. Glenn Engman is a master color printer. His work compliments my images throughout this book. ■ *The Third Eye* marks a turning point in my life. I am grateful to my Creator for a long prosperous career in still photography and for the fun I've had seeing with my third eye.

Béla Kalman   February, 1994